Table of Contents

Introduction: The Most Important Question of Your Life

Chapter 1: The Invisible Roads Your Life Is Taking

Chapter 2: Your Deserving Origins

Chapter 3: The Endless Chain Reaction of Your Pain

Chapter 4: Meet The People Controlling Your Life

Chapter 5: Flip The Switch: Taking Back Your Happiness

Chapter 6: Six Steps To Protect Your Self Worth

Conclusion: Your True Power

Introduction

The Most Important Question of Your Life

D o you ever look around at friends, family, colleagues, or the people you grew up with and wonder why their lives appear to be more successful than yours?

Do you find yourself comparing and despairing, feeling that you don't quite measure up, while others seem to be so happy, peaceful, and in control?

Maybe your old friend from the neighborhood has a top-notch job while yours doesn't satisfy you at all. Or your younger brother is happily married while you can't find a partner. Perhaps your college roommate is living the lifestyle you crave, while you're still struggling with car payments.

Do you ever think, *It isn't fair. Why not me?*

After all, you started out with the same social and economic advantages they had. You worked hard, maybe even harder, yet success came to them instead of you.

So why are others thriving in their work, in their relationships, and in their leisure time, while you grind through each day overwhelmed by stress and exhaustion? Do you wonder why you often feel stuck yet everybody else seems happy? And you may be successful in many ways, but are still comparing yourselves to others, feeling you are never enough. Your mindset is constantly reminding you that you are not at your full potential.

If so, this book is for you, and I want to assure you right now that you are not alone.

I've spent decades reading self-help books, enrolling in coaching courses, visiting therapists, traveling to seminars, and studying with "gurus" and "thought leaders," all in a quest to answer the painful question about why my life isn't where it's supposed to be.

I was driven to do all of this because I felt dissatisfied with my own accomplishments in comparison to those of others. So I kept searching for an answer about the anatomy of success and achievement.

I would finish one self-help book and compulsively turn to another; or come home from a motivational seminar bursting with enthusiasm for the vital new information I'd just received, excited about how to apply it to my life. Surely, *this* was the magic ingredient that would make all the difference.

I'd set my goals, apply the methods I'd learned, follow through on the action steps, and then... only *some* progress or nothing at all.

This discouraged and disheartened me. All I could think about was the enthusiasm and sense of hope that had motivated me only days or weeks before, and the dejected feeling now because I didn't accomplish what I had set out to do.

I would lie awake at night, wondering what missing link was causing me to stay stuck in life when other people seemed to move forward and succeed. I reminded myself that I had a successful business, people who loved me, and the respect of my colleagues. Yet it was not enough. I felt so strongly that my life should be further advanced by now.

Indeed, as a doctor working with patients every day in my Manhattan office, I'd seen both physical and emotional transformations in hundreds, perhaps thousands of lives. I'd also traveled the world, sharing success stories from my practice with other professionals, many of whom achieved greater success, happiness, and peace of mind because of what I had taught them. This is not about being a failure. This is about recognizing your current position is far from where you want to be and know it could be.

Admittedly, many of my clients did *not* experience positive change. And I constantly wondered, *what is the difference between these two groups of people?* One would use what I taught and see incredible results and accomplishments, while the other would stay stuck, spinning their wheels in self-sabotage with little to no change.

The explanation for why some people succeed and others do not was buried in one of those two groups. This very same understanding also applies to why some people succeed, yet achievement never feels good enough. I was compelled to find it.

So I immersed myself in studying the lives of friends and colleagues in an attempt to discover the source of these striking differences. I was able to rule out skill level, work ethic, education, background, desire, or focus as the *underlying* reason. All of the things that society defined as the "keys to success" were actually different for each person.

The people who were struggling and unhappy often worked just as hard, if not harder, than the others. They had the same skills and education, and the same desire for success. Yet something profound made all the difference between success and failure.

Whether you are successful or are just scraping by, you recognize there is something deeply different in others who have what you are striving to get. And it seems to come so easily to them, and not you, even though you have the same basic start. What is the factor that is holding you back and not them?

As I interviewed men and women and poured through the data I'd collected, I started seeing a trend. It was subtle at first, but then I began to see that the people who'd been the most successful didn't spend much time *thinking about it*. They just *did it*.

Achieving their goals was simply part of their DNA, their core belief system. That's when I realized that as helpful as traditional self-improvement books and courses can be, the missing link could never be found there.

The defining secret—the answer to the question I've posed—influences every aspect of your life, from romantic relationships (or lack thereof), to your bank account, your physical health, and whether you feel optimistic and inspired, or fried and frustrated.

It determines *exactly* what you're able to create and have.

Know this: *No matter how much knowledge you possess or how hard you work, you will never reach your goals without this one important piece in place.*

When you find the one piece that's missing, you won't be required to work any harder, set more precise goals, or recite formulaic affirmations.

The crucial determining ingredient that I'm going to share with you will help you instantly recognize whether you have it or not. My hope is that once you reactivate this trait you will never again feel stuck, exhausted, or tempted to give up.

* * * * *

I'll never forget the day I finally discovered the missing link between those who succeed and those who don't. I was meeting a friend in New York City, named Jayson (you'll meet him in Chapter 4). Besides being an exceedingly successful entrepreneur and business owner with decades of impressive experience, Jayson has been equally successful in every area of his life, despite being raised in a modest family in Queens, without any privileges.

As I pressed Jayson for answers about his accomplishments over lunch, he finally said, " I've never really thought about the reason for my success. I always just believed I *deserved* it."

Time stopped. I don't even remember what else Jayson said during that lunch, because in that moment I finally *got it*. With one word, I had an epiphany, and it turned out that the answer had always been right there in front of me. Jayson's passing comment was the illumination I had been looking for.

Your reality is a reflection of what you truly believe you deserve in your life.

Jayson didn't even know he was living according to this principle. In fact, most successful men and women don't realize it either. The premise of their belief that they were going to be successful regardless of their circumstances is deep-rooted and subconscious. But every action they take and the results they get in life are nonetheless a result of this underlying deserving belief, and it drives everything forward.

As I soon learned this, it became clear that a deserving (or undeserving) state of mind transmits signals to the entire world around you, dramatically affecting your success rate and ultimate destiny. As psychiatrist Sir David Hawkins says: "People simply mirror back your internal belief systems."

People who have exactly what they want unhesitatingly feel that they *deserve* to have it, and they convey this in their confidence, words, and actions. This is true across all areas of life, including personal relationships, physical health, career trajectory, material possessions, and overall peace of mind and happiness.

Those with a "deserving mentality" trust fully that they are entitled to a high level of satisfaction in their lives, and this belief actually *creates* that reality (conversely, if you don't believe you deserve what you want, you'll never get it).

As I thought back on my research and all the patients, friends, colleagues, and family members I had interviewed, it seemed to be obviously true.

I realized that Jayson had hit on the common denominator for those with fulfilling lives. But even in the same family, one successful sibling didn't guarantee the same level of achievement for the other. As I saw, there was often a stark difference between those who enjoyed a lifetime of success and happiness, and those who seemed to struggle endlessly.

The contrast between the people who have what they want and those who don't could not be more vivid. **Deep down, the group who stayed stuck, burned-out, and frustrated did not believe they deserved to have what they most desired.** Their yearning was real and very powerful. They often worked very hard to achieve a goal, sacrificing much along the way. But the journey was doomed from the start because the only reality they had created was one of *undeserving*.

Once I digested all this and could see the profound value of deservedness, I created a simple method to reliably test your own *deserving mentality*.

* * * * *

Take a moment to think about an area of your life where you are experiencing frustration, disappointment, or feeling stuck. Maybe it is a broken relationship, or lacking the loving, fulfilling relationship you've longed for but have not experienced. Perhaps it's the home you dream of, or the enriching, satisfying career that seems out of reach.

No area of your life is off-limits for this exercise, so pick the one that's most meaningful and hold it in your mind.

Get very quiet for a moment, and then gently form the following question in your mind about the result you desire:

"Do I *truly* believe I deserve having this in my life?"

If your mind instantly says, "no," congratulations! This is a clear, unambiguous answer explaining why you don't have your desired goal. The journey before you will be filled with intriguing discoveries as you learn the simple, but powerful methods I share in these pages ahead.

If you answered "yes," there could be an even greater challenge. True, you are being honest when you say, "I want X, Y or Z." Your desire *is* focused and strong. But in your subconscious mind—the deepest and most powerful part of your psyche—there may be resistance that can sabotage your success.

Why?

Your subconscious isn't sophisticated or even logical. It's a primal part of your brain that stores your deepest emotions and impulses. It is the automatic feelings, responses, and urges that guide your every action. It hears your stated desire, but it instantly objects, saying "You don't deserve this."

It's a battle you can never win, because your attempt to feel deserving conflicts with the stronger message that you are *not*. And if you don't truly believe to your core that you deserve happiness or success, then it's impossible to create it. So if you answered "yes" to my question, your journey may be more challenging than if you said no. And you may have to work harder to overcome your internal denial.

Right about now you might be thinking to yourself, "I know I deserve it, so whatever is going on in my subconscious mind can't really be the cause of my unhappiness."

I understand your skepticism. But scientists have proven the correlation between what your mind creates and the reality you experience. Likewise, physicians have demonstrated the relationship between a mind expecting pain or disease and the presence of those in the body.

If your mind has that kind of power over the physical world, why couldn't it just as effectively use that power in a more positive way? **If your mind can create pain and disease, why couldn't you use that same power to create wellness and happiness?**

These truths are not just found in laboratory experiments and research journals. In the first chapter, you will understand exactly what it feels like to have a deserving belief. You'll meet Dr. Anderson, who quadrupled his income and essentially eliminated stress in his life through the application of one simple but revolutionary process.

In chapter 2, we delve into the origin of your undeserving beliefs and learn why traditional approaches to personal development, goal setting, coaching, therapy, and even meditation get the most important things wrong.

In chapter 3, you'll understand how undeserving beliefs show up in the most important areas of your life, and how applying my process helped one business owner add $25,000 in *monthly* personal income after learning this principle.

In chapter 4, you'll see how undeserving beliefs evolved in your past. You'll read the extraordinary and true story of how a single conversation overheard by a young child 30 years ago defined an entire lifetime.

In chapter 5, you'll read about *The Deserving Process*, which will help you move powerfully toward the life you dream of. You'll also learn—

probably for the first time—the truth about the most powerful emotion in your life.

In chapter 6, you'll be introduced to my best tools for strengthening your deserving beliefs. These are the exact methods I teach to people around the world who have seen incredible results. All together, I've packed a lifetime of study, observation, and analysis into this book.

Make this book personal. Highlight, underline, write in the margins, and use the online resources I have provided, which are only accessible to you. Take advantage of every opportunity this book gives to you, because this is YOUR life we are talking about. This book is your personal guide to navigating your life, changing the conditions of it so you ultimately end up where you want to be.

Let's start right now. Take a moment to breathe in and out deeply, and ask yourself these two questions:

What in my life do I want to change the most? What will that outcome look like?

Try this visualization as a guide:

Picture that new house and look closely at the color of the brick, the style of the windows, the grain of the wood floors, and the beauty of the backyard.

Now reflect on your thoughts as you finish a workday in a career that you love, knowing that you've made an extraordinary difference in the lives of others.

What do you smell as you stroll on the beach during your ideal getaway? How do you feel as you sit across the table from your lover, your partner, your best friend, gazing into his or her eyes, knowing that this person loves you and desires everything for you that you want for yourself? Where in your body do you feel that?

Feel these things right now. Would you like those feelings to last?

It's totally possible. And I'm going to show you how to sustain that kind of positivity and certainty in all areas of your life.

Know this… your current beliefs have created the life you have right now. If your circumstances are disappointing, then your undeserving beliefs are keeping you bound to your current life.

But when you change your subconscious belief from undeserving to deserving, a new pathway will unfold for you. When you believe you deserve what you envision, you'll naturally take new actions to bring it closer. The results will be different now because you are different *internally*. You'll find that more and more, life's magical serendipities and circumstances will align to present you with the people and opportunities that will help you reach your goals.

When your deserving belief is *switched on*, everything starts moving in the direction you want it to go. Money, time, and love are no longer in short supply. The body we'd like, the job of our dreams, the ideal mate and the perfect circle of friends are all within our reach. Barriers fall away, negative self-talk diminishes, procrastination and exhaustion disappear, and previously unimagined opportunities present themselves.

In short, having the life you want IS within your control when you're in possession of the most important and final piece of the puzzle: **Believing you deserve having it.**

Chapter 1

The Invisible Roads Your Life Is Taking

On a beautiful spring evening in New York, just before the sun crept behind the skyscrapers, I raced off on my bike for a joyride. It was the end of a long, busy day at the office taking care of patients and now I was ready to relax and enjoy the balmy weather.

Amidst the cabs honking and the thick rush-hour traffic, there I was pedaling down 71st street past the majestic St. James Church. If you'd seen me, I was overdressed for biking in my dress pants, leather shoes, and button down shirt. But it didn't matter. I was enjoying every minute of it.

I loved the sensation of the setting sun warming my face and the gentle breeze blowing through my hair. All the while, as I wove through traffic, I was energized listening to my favorite '80s one-hit wonders blasting through my earphones. All of it amounted to the simplest sense of joy.

I took a sharp right onto Park Avenue heading southbound toward the MetLife Building, which towers over NYC's historic Grand Central Station. After a couple of blocks of fast pedaling I finally reached the point where Park Ave starts to descend. Now I could coast while increasing speed.

Block after block I caught the green lights, with no stops, as I flowed along with the cabs, feeling at one with the city. And through it all, I took in the fragrance of the springtime air. Nothing could beat it.

If you had taken a picture of me at this moment, you would have seen a subtle grin soaking it all up. In that moment, I thought to myself, what in the world could be better than appreciating everything around me?

When I finally hit a red light I took the time to turn to my right and observe the parade of harried office workers pouring out of skyscrapers as they battled rush-hour traffic and the clogged sidewalks to get to the subway. Their long workday was finally over. They looked pretty beaten down.

In fact, what I saw in their faces was grim. Not one person was smiling. There wasn't a hint of joy or enthusiasm. No laughter or camaraderie. Instead, there was just a sea of expressionless downcast eyes, locked on their cellphones, everyone in their own thoughts. It was a blur of cold, stern faces, lost in the commotion, seemingly unable to enjoy the beauty of a spring night. Everyone looked so tense and stressed out by a robotic routine that clearly weighed heavily on them.

In that moment I knew something was very wrong. How could this army of competent professionals be outside in the most fascinating city in the world and still manage to look so glum and disinterested?

Surely they must have been grateful for *something*? How about the endless opportunities this magnificent city has to offer, whether it was the museums, parks, restaurants, Broadway shows, or the countless options for socializing and entertainment? And where was their excitement about returning home to their families after a long day at work? None of it seemed to matter.

So in that moment on my bike, when all of these thoughts were whirling through my head, I had an epiphany—instantly knowing what was most important in life for me.

It wasn't just the wellbeing of my patients, or the development of my practice, or finding the right mate, or earning enough money. All those things were important. But on this night I actually found my calling—my purpose and passion.

It was the conviction that my destiny was to contribute to others by nurturing their peace of mind, their ability to enjoy the world and make a difference too. Specifically, I could help them realize that they *deserved* to be happy and successful. And I could teach them how to activate a sense of deservedness that would unlock the secrets to fulfillment.

In the years to follow, I would coach and mentor doctors and professionals from more than 18 countries using a technique you'll read about here which allows you to create your deserving belief.

This, in turn, leads to success in all areas of your life. Through it all, I found there was one common denominator amongst everyone I met: that we all yearn to be happy, to live in harmony, and to realize our potential. And we all need a helping hand. And I offer it to you here in this book.

* * * * *

After 14 years in private practice, Dr. John Anderson was burnt out. From a financial point of view, he was barely making ends meet. So he often worried about what his future would look like if things didn't get any better.

Retirement was certainly nowhere in sight.

True, he was able to pay his bills at the end of each month, but he still owed the majority of his graduate school loans. Unfortunately, his monthly payment was just covering the cost of the interest. At this current payback rate there was no end in sight for repaying those loans.

Because of this situation, his weekends with his wife and children were filled with angst and anxiety. It seemed that he was always obsessing about whether or not new patients would call during the next week and how many would return to see him.

All of these worried thoughts distracted him from being able to truly enjoy his free time outside of work. Clearly, this was not the life Dr. Anderson envisioned. And inwardly, he constantly doubted if he had made the right career choice.

Overall, the embarrassment and self-doubt he felt was so strong that he hid all this from his wife, including the fact that he had hired me to work with him as his coach. Had he confided this information he believed that she would have chastised him. After all, the other coaches he had seen in the past had not made a bit of difference. So she would have felt that the money spent was once again wasted.

When we began working together, we first dove into the question:

"Do I *truly* believe I deserve a better, more prosperous life?"

The answer to this was critical to getting new results for Dr. Anderson. From the start, I sensed that beneath his attempts to create a more successful practice were subconscious beliefs about himself that were holding him back. In other words, his undeserving belief about the potential success of his practice had led to self-sabotage. So regardless of what he said or did when it came to patient care and his practice's growth, nothing improved.

Together we took an honest look into his personal history. Most often we bury deep within our psyche our most hurtful memories. Dr. Anderson admitted that growing up, he had a very pessimistic father who gave negative advice on everything from dating to classroom grades to his athletics.

When he told his father his desire to become a doctor, he received the usual pessimistic response because it was certainly outside the cultural norms of the family. His father's response was, "John, we're blue-collar people.

That's not for us."

In that moment, those two toxic, self-limiting sentences planted an undeserving seed in John. Over the next 30 years, they sabotaged his career, dramatically affecting his income and the life he could provide for his wife and children, not to mention the damage to his peace of mind.

In short, he'd never forgotten the sentences spoken by his father. They were burned deep into his youthful psyche and became his driving beliefs as an adult. He never realized it until we started working together.

It's important to note that Dr. Anderson's father had no idea how negatively his words had affected his son. Nor did he have any self-awareness of the pessimism he had expressed throughout his son's upbringing. The rationale? His father was just being himself, the only way he knew how to be, oblivious to the psychological impact he had on others. Dr. Anderson's father was only repeating what had been bestowed upon him during his own upbringing. He then passed that belief system onto his son.

Now, after we worked together, he became aware of how powerfully those two sentences had affected his life and career and he believed he could reverse them. In fact, he said he could see his "practice exploding" (in a good way) with new patients and profits just as soon as he let his undeserving beliefs go. Before this awareness, he could never have ever envisioned such stellar success in his work.

With a new vision and optimism of what was possible, Dr. Anderson committed to doing **The Deserving Process**, a simple three-step exercise he could practice from the comfort of his own home or office daily. Within days, he started feeling better about himself. In fact, months later he was paying himself four times as much as when we first started working together. And he accomplished this putting in fewer hours at the office, with less marketing expenses, and reduced stress. Overnight, he loved showing up at the office every day. The dread was gone.

* * * * *

Somewhere from our own youth, we all have experienced what Dr. Anderson did—*the feeling of not being good enough, of not belonging, or fitting in, or something being intrinsically wrong with us.*

Most often it is an unintentional inherited falsehood from our parents. They didn't know they did it to you. It's the last thing they ever would have wanted to happen. But it happened anyway.

No one gets out of childhood unscathed no matter how privileged their upbringing may be or how loving their parents were. Whether it was your mother or father, a teacher or preacher, grandparents, or close friends—each of them affected you in a myriad of ways. There are specific moments from your earliest memories that literally define what you believe you are capable of having and achieving. **Your history leaves no mystery.** It's exactly where your deserving—or undeserving—beliefs are first formed.

Certain life events cause a metaphorical switch to be flipped inside your mind that either sabotages you from having what you want in life or gives you the ability to create it.

In short, undeserving beliefs are learned. They show up in any area of your life—in your work, your relationships with family and friends, and in your marriage too. This includes your personal finances, health, and overall attitude and life outlook.

How often have you felt as if you're never going to catch a break financially? You've never been able to get out of debt or earn an income you feel truly proud of. Or: You might earn all the money you need but you're still feeling competitive and deprived, always looking at what your colleagues or neighbors have and feeling you're not enough.

When it comes to physical health, feeling undeserving can show up in a variety of ways. You have difficulty staying on a diet and maintaining a healthy weight. Or maybe you're bouncing around from doctor to doctor not being able to figure out the source of your chronic pain. In romantic relationships, it can be manifested in relationships painfully ending over and over, year after year. Or maybe you're already in a relationship, but are feeling stuck or bored, with far less love, fulfillment, peace and happiness than you crave.

Every single area of your life is influenced by your deserving or undeserving beliefs.

Let's go deeper: What does the term 'deserving belief' actually mean? It's your conscious and, more importantly, subconscious belief about what you're ENTITLED to—anywhere in your life. It affects every one of your attitudes. Your attitudes form your actions, the words you speak, and the vision you hold in your mind of your future. All of these factors create the wealth, health, and position you have in life. **So at its essence, the level of your deservedness mirrors what you have in your life at any given moment.**

Even if you don't yet have what you want in life, a deserving belief gives you the confidence and certainty that it's coming. You have no doubt you're taking the steps to create it. **With that deserving belief in yourself, procrastination and fear melt away.** You know in your heart that you are both responsible for and capable of creating the life you want.

* * * * *

There are two crucial components to the question "Do You Truly Believe You Deserve Your Ideal Life?" Let's look at each one separately so you're clear on the concept:
- Believe
- Deserve

It's easy to *believe* that what you want in life is *possible*. How often have we heard the common jargon:*"If you can visualize what you want with clarity and specificity, then it can manifest in your life."* But is a vision alone sufficient? After all, just knowing it's doable does not mean it's in the realm of your reality. And that is all that really counts—*you actually having the life you want.*

So inherently knowing what's available in this world does not mean that you personally <u>believe</u> you deserve to have it. This is a major distinction. In fact, it's common to have such low self-esteem that you believe everyone else is deserving of what you want, but not you. And that's one crucial stumbling block to getting what you want.

You may believe it is *possible* to have something—as in one day far off in the future. Maybe it will happen if you get lucky, like winning the lottery or keeping your head down, working hard 16 hours a day for years.

A true deserving belief means you know you're worthy of having it in your life **right now**. And if you're feeling deprived of what you want, it's only because you likely don't believe you deserve it. *Otherwise it would be there.*

Conversely, you feel you have success coming to you and you are already grateful, knowing it is going to happen. There's tremendous power in the attitude of gratitude, felt in advance of your dream being manifested. You'll see how that works later when you learn The Deserving Process.

In part two of the deserving question, you must know that fulfilling your dream has NOTHING to do with your skin color, age, gender, ethnicity, socioeconomic background, religion, education, or sexual orientation. What side of the tracks you grew up on does not matter. No matter what, you have the God-given right of deserving what this world has to offer. No one is excluded.

By the way, the word "worthy" isn't a direct synonym for deserving, as worthiness can be exclusionary. Are only some people worthy of happiness, endowed with a blessing from some authority figure or deity? No. If you ever see that, disregard it and move on. Deserving is entirely your choice. No authority outside of yourself decides if you're worthy, entitled to, or deserving of your dream or not. Knowing this is extremely powerful because you realize you are in control of your future.

I'm not saying your background has NO influence on the trajectory of your success. Do your life circumstances play a role in making it harder to achieve certain goals? Certainly. Are there thousands of innocent babies born today who will one day feel either deserving or undeserving, depending upon their parents and environment? Absolutely. Some of them will have a greater head start on success than others.

In fact, at an early age, everything that happens to them will dictate which conclusion about themselves they make. But now, years later, you can transform your belief, knowing at the most fundamental level that you are deserving of what life has to offer.

There is no inherent genetic, familial history or any other factor that dictates at conception that you are not deserving of what is available in the world for you at birth.

But what if you cannot even imagine what your ideal life looks like? You're stuck in a 9 to 6 job, rushing home to prepare dinner, taking care of your children, ending the day exhausted and dissatisfied, only to repeat the cycle the next day. On weekends, there's never-ending housework to do, errands to run, and children's needs to fulfill.

Feeling trapped at work and at home leaves you feeling unable to create a future that inspires. Having come this far in life, you figure, if I haven't yet created it for myself, how will I ever do it?

This inability to envision a future that inspires is not because you're too busy. It's not even because you do not have the know-how. It's because your undeserving beliefs are driving you. These self-sabotaging thoughts cause you to feel stuck and overwhelmed—and you wind up in a state of procrastination, exhaustion, or even hopelessness.

* * * * *

Contrary to a widespread belief that everyone should be motivated to escape from negative states of mind and pursue their wellbeing, for many people, it's not even a thought. You're like a robot, going through the motions of life without even thinking about what you deserve and how it might impact your happiness and life circumstances.

Indeed, according to research on mood and self-esteem, people who feel undeserving lack the motivation to make things better for themselves.[1] As it turns out, when experiencing a personal loss or failure, people with low self-esteem are likely to believe that they don't deserve to feel better. So they're willing to accept their suffering as inevitable, even well-deserved. What?! The reason for this peculiar self-destructive tendency is simple: our subconscious need for justice is stronger than our will to be happy.

It's like we are continuously re-evaluating our own level of deserving, looking through the prism of low self-esteem. In the end, we have a monumental choice: We are either motivated to stay in a miserable condition or to change it. If we stay stuck, the sad events we experience justify our perception of our own undeservingness.

Driven by undeserving thoughts, we continuously evaluate how much *others* deserve. The more positive characteristics other people possess, and the more honorable and likable they are, the more we feel that they deserve desirable outcomes.[2] **We compare and despair, applying our distorted attitudes toward** ourselves.

If you see yourself in the research, it's OK. We all fall victim to the workings of the human mind, which is more often operating to survive rather than thrive. In the next section you're going to be able to identify exactly where your undeserving beliefs are in the most important areas of your life, and what can be done to change them.

* * * * *

WHERE EXACTLY ARE *YOUR* UNDESERVING BELIEFS?

Building my private practice from scratch didn't happen easily. Six months after getting my doctorate in Chiropractic I still hadn't opened an office. I was paralyzed by indecision and fear over every aspect of starting a practice, from where it should be located to exactly how it should be run.

Much of my anxiety stemmed from my first year in graduate school. I attended a seminar hosted by a number of doctors in thriving practices and connected with one in particular who had his office near where I grew up in New York. He asked me where I wanted to practice and what I intended my future fees to be. Huh? I had no clue! I was just a freshman. But as I stumbled around, whatever I told him caused him to respond: *"Then you can't practice in New York. You'll have to stay in the South."*

These words stayed with me for the next three years of school. I was born and raised in New York, attended NYU, and all my family and friends were here. It was the only way of life I really knew. But this doctor had put a doubt in my mind that activated an undeserving thought deep within me. I soon began searching for a new location in the South to start life after graduation, merely based upon his discouraging words.

In short, hearing those meaningless two sentences implanted within me an undeserving belief that practicing back home in New York would be impossible. **There was no malicious intent on the doctor's part, rather a candid reply based on *his* beliefs.** He was not trying to sabotage my mentality or future. *Yet that's exactly what happened.*

It wasn't long after that that I visited Charleston, South Carolina and fell in love with its beauty. For the next few years, I often visited and researched the city with full intention to move there after graduation.

When I finally arrived in Charleston armed with my degree, nothing felt right about starting a practice. I woke up every day filled with anxiety, my heart pounding. I was a nervous wreck. I had no appetite and hardly ate. I drove around all day helplessly, unable to find a practice space that inspired me to sign a lease. Even neighbors I introduced myself to commented, "Why are you coming here?"

Finally, with no inclination of where I wanted to practice, I admitted I was not meant to be there at all and gave up, retreating back to New York with my tail between my legs. I moved in with my mother, with only $3,000 in the bank and started up a home project, painting the inside of her house as a distraction from taking steps forward in my career.

At that point, the only thing I *did* know was that I wanted to be close to my family. Within six months, I started a practice from scratch on one of the most expensive blocks in all of Manhattan, still with just a few thousand dollars to my name. I felt at peace being back in New York, even though I had made no preparations for the transition. Instead of basing my decision to move from an undeserving perspective, I forged ahead with a plan to succeed, knowing that New York was where I was meant to be.

We all have deserving beliefs in every area of our lives. Intellectually, we may know our belief is not true, but it still controls our thoughts and actions. In order to change a pattern in any area of your life, you must gain clarity about what your deserving beliefs are and are not. Only then can you do something about each one. **If you don't become aware of your undeserving beliefs, they will dictate the rest of your life.**

There are two categories of people on the undeserving spectrum. You are in the first group if you can see and admit your undeserving belief. Maybe you can even pinpoint where the belief originated. In any case, you're aware of it.

The other group is oblivious to the idea that they even have undeserving beliefs. They might just feel as if bad luck was the cause of being stuck. In other words, they feel victimized rather than realizing that they themselves are the cause of any limitation. If this group better describes you, instead of analyzing your luck, take a look at your beliefs (which is never easy) and understand how those negative messages have held you back.

If you look deep into your past, there will always be recurring themes of self-sabotage based upon an undeserving belief. You may not realize it or admit it's self-obstruction, but if the same result is happening over and over again in different circumstances, it is an internal problem, not an external one. You don't have to understand how you self-sabotage, just acknowledge that it is indeed happening.

To help, I've devised a simple, two-part question to target which group you are in so you have clear direction how to overcome your undeserving beliefs and flip your switch.

You have two responses possible when you ask yourself: "Do I Truly Believe I Deserve Having This in My Life?" If your answer is a NO, then you acknowledge you have an undeserving belief. However, knowing you have an underserving belief will not change anything for you. Doing The Deserving Process you learn in chapter 5 will change it.

If you answer YES, then objectively assess if you are steadily moving towards your goal with predictability. It's progress, not perfection. You will get there if you keep doing what you're doing. You are on your way even though it is not present right now. If this applies to you, move on to another area of your life that is not yet fully realized or soon to be and develop your deserving belief there.

However, if you notice that your self-sabotaging behaviors are not changing, keeping you stuck even though you say you deserve what you want, then subconsciously you do have an undeserving belief. It's blocking your path toward progress. And that's okay. That's exactly what you are here to change. Sometimes it is not so easy to assess whether or not we are making real progress toward our goals ...

Goals relating to numbers are easiest to predict potential outcomes. But what about something not as tangible or quantitative, like love and romance? That's not exactly predictable. *Is it?* Yes and no.

If you are looking at romantic relationships and you believe you *are* deserving of what you want, but you're still single and alone, then you must be demonstrating behaviors divergent from your goal.

If you were consistently in the wrong relationships and now you are choosing not to enter into those same patterns, that is an indication things are changing for you. Or perhaps after years of staying in an unhealthy marriage, you finally stood up for yourself and left. Or if you chose to stay in the relationship, you're now dealing with your marital issues, the result being a clear change in the energy and emotion of that relationship.

If you observe that your tendency to self-sabotage is lessening, then you are making progress. It doesn't guarantee you will get the result you are after, but at least you are not stuck in the same hamster-wheel set of circumstances you had been in. **Removing your sabotaging behaviors is just as important as adding the right behaviors on your way toward your desire and goal.**

However, if no matter how hard you try, it's clear that nothing is improving, and it feels like Groundhog Day for years on end, you do not have a deserving belief in this area of your life. For instance, maybe you've vowed to earn more and save more, but you've nonetheless seen no substantial increase in your income or ability to put money away. Or, despite attempts at dieting, you've seen no improvement in your body size or weight. If this is you, then subconsciously you do NOT *truly believe you deserve having the results you say you want.*

But do not despair. Realization and awareness is always the first step. It is never too late to do something about it, which is the entire purpose of starting The Deserving Process.

* * * * *

There's nothing more important in your life than peace of mind. But what leads to it is different for everyone, just as success manifests itself differently for each person. However, when you're missing what you most want, it's impossible to feel truly fulfilled. No one can *give* you peace of mind. You can't buy it, and you can't depend on somebody else to provide it for you.

Peace of mind is an ongoing state of happiness, gratitude, and contentment about your current life, a state driven from optimistic expectation for your future. If you don't believe you deserve peace of mind, it doesn't matter what any other part of your life looks like; you won't have it. If you are not experiencing daily peace of mind, you need to look at your undeserving beliefs.

Every single one of us could have more love, joy, gratitude, and fulfillment in all areas of our lives. But it is up to you whether you experience each as often as you'd like. **Believing you deserve peace of mind throughout your life is just as important as any other area you're focused on creating.** That is what I want for you and believe you deserve.

Make sure to do the workbook exercise at the end of the chapter and visit the online bonus videos exclusively for you.

Most Important Chapter 1 Takeaways

- Your life as it is right now is a direct reflection of your past and current deserving beliefs.
- We all develop deserving beliefs at some point in our lives. We may be very successful in one area, but just cannot get it right in another; i.e. extremely successful in business, but can never meet the "right" person and have a healthy and happy relationship. The objective is to realize where and why the undeserving beliefs are and how to move past them.
- An undeserving belief can be planted in you from a single experience and then build throughout your life, continually reinforcing itself.
- Undeserving belief does not encompass your entire life; it applies separately to each specific area.
- Undeserving does NOT equal unworthy.
- Undeserving beliefs are your choice to change.
- Feeling stuck in life is a direct symptom of an undeserving belief.
- No matter how successful you may currently be, you can still have undeserving beliefs keeping you from greater accomplishment or causing the results in the less successful areas of your life.

Chapter 2

Your Deserving Origins

As I built a successful private practice from scratch on Manhattan's Upper East Side, I saw a dire need from fellow practitioners for the practice growth resources I could provide. Running a doctor's office was getting tougher for both providers and patients as medical insurance declined coverage or disappeared altogether, leaving many patients with no ability to get covered treatment.

I decided to create an online coaching program, which has now been used by hundreds of doctors in over 18 countries and counting. The goal? Grow private practices delivering an exceptional patient experience, in which patients feel truly listened to and respected.

As a result of my program I've been grateful to receive countless testimonials from doctors, some of whom have been in practice for more than forty years. Prior to the coaching many of them had felt stuck in old patterns, feeling burnt out, anxious, and even fearful. But all that had changed. The end result was that these practitioners had enhanced the quality of care while growing a business, which led to an improved lifestyle.

However, the material I share with you in this book is not exclusive to doctors. I've given the same concepts to people of all walks of life and career paths, both beginners and those already in established careers.

During this time, while providing each coaching recipient the same instruction, I discovered that the real difference between those who stayed stuck compared to the ones who experienced growth was whether he or she BELIEVED they <u>deserved</u> the success they sought. And, their amount of *un*deserving belief is what determined their degree of self-sabotage. If you've used coaching, goal setting, or other means for achievement or changing your life, have you ended up experiencing any of the following?

You didn't fully learn and apply the resources you were provided: If you do not believe you are deserving of an outcome, the information you are given simply won't be taken as seriously or applied correctly.

You procrastinate: Never beginning or making real progress toward your goal.

You are in denial: You believe you are doing everything you can to change your life circumstances. But, if the people closest to you are asked if you're making an effort, they'd shake their head in disagreement.

You feel overwhelmed or stuck: Not asking for help or answers along the way. Excuses for not asking for an answer stop you.

Your fear of failure stops you: Both the personal feeling of failure and looking like a failure to others prevents you from pursuing your goals.

You don't have a vision for your future: *If you don't have clarity about what you want your life to look like there's no possibility to get there.* Undeserving beliefs cause your lack of vision.

Your results go up and down: Good months follow bad months endlessly. There's no consistency, and you lose what you have created just as quickly as you got it. This is a result of not maintaining steady progress because of undeserving beliefs influencing self-sabotage.

You've never achieved results you intended in the past: You enroll in program after program and coach after coach and nothing ever changes. It is not that all of these past resources didn't provide value. It is your self-sabotaging undeserving beliefs holding you back.

Your results are never good enough: You actually see the growth and progress you seek, but as soon as you reach your goals you immediately place yourself at the first step of a new, loftier one. You do not appreciate and acknowledge what you do have in your life. You are always looking for more or better, *resulting in little to no long-term happiness or fulfillment.*

* * * * *

As humans, we all have similar mentalities. We are wired to want more and want what we do not have. And, we all want the most valuable and cherished emotions and experiences—to love and be loved, deep fulfillment, happiness, and peace of mind.

If you're taking the time to read this book you've likely already read other books in this same genre. Maybe you've also attended personal growth seminars, done online courses, or created a vision board. However, if you do not see your life changing it's likely due to undeserving beliefs you have acquired.

The traditional mediums for personal growth can rarely flip your switch from undeserving to deserving for two reasons:
1. Self-help seminars, coaches and resources are often unaware of the "undeserving" concept.
2. Even if they are, your ability to digest their instruction is flawed. Why? Because you're receiving the information through your undeserving filter, causing self-sabotage using and acting on the material to get the results you want.

Before lasting results can take effect, primary is your deserving belief. If your belief is not present, the best coaches, mentors, and therapists with the perfect plan will not get you where you want to go, even if your mentors have done it for themselves. Even if they have helped thousands just like you use the same process, *it still won't work for you* if your deserving belief is missing.

Here are the most common methods for growth and achievement and why they will most often fail you if you have an undeserving belief. My intention is not to bash each of these common resources. Each of these makes getting what you want far easier if your deserving belief *is present*. That is the only caveat. Without it, they will rarely be able to benefit you.

Goal Setting

Setting goals and expectations of what you want your future to look like has tremendous value. It gives you benchmarks to see how you're doing and a purpose to strive toward as you create the life you want. I recommend always having goals to work toward in your life. However, the traditional notion of goal setting can often produce more harm to your psyche than good. This sounds counter-intuitive, but it's true.

Goal setting (and achieving) can be one of the most demoralizing parts of your entire life, contributing to unhappiness and lack of peace of mind, *even if you do reach your goals*. **What matters most is why you set your goals and the way in which you go about achieving them.**

Here is my experience with goal setting: It wasn't until my sixth month in practice that I started finally seeing bottom-line profits, ones that I was proud of. I will never forget Cinco De Mayo in my first year of practice. I was rushing through my April profit-and-loss accounting before racing downtown to meet friends for a fun night out in Manhattan.

By the end, calculating all my overhead costs and revenue, I saw $20,000 in profit the month prior. I had never made that much in a single month in my life (perhaps even in a year). Before starting my practice, I only had part-time and summer jobs like pizza delivery, summer maintenance at my high school (mainly because the head basketball coach was the boss, which meant extra-long lunches shooting hoops in the gym with him), pool maintenance, and working for doctor offices' doing new patient marketing. Seeing that amount of profit, I felt a real sense of accomplishment and pride. This great feeling stuck with me the entire night out as I partied with my friends.

But when I woke the next day, that happiness was already gone. The pride and satisfaction had quickly turned to anxiety and pressure. It had taken a lot of work to achieve those financial results. And I thought if I didn't keep up that effort, I likely wouldn't reach those numbers again. Worse, if I didn't meet or exceed $20,000 profit, I would feel like a failure as my business was declining.

So on the morning of May 6, as I was 20 percent of the way through the month, I didn't know if I was on course to meet or exceed the profit I had reached. *I already felt behind.* And rather than happiness, all I could feel was a pit in my stomach. I didn't have any faith that I would maintain the progress I had made.

This is the story of traditional goal setting. And it never ends, no matter how often you accomplish your goals or how large the successes may be. The vast majority of us set goals that overwhelm us and cause paralysis or exhaustion along the way. We generally don't reach our goals and, instead, wind up feeling discouraged or like a failure.

If you are among the small percentage of those who do accomplish our goal, you feel great for about fifteen minutes to two days, before the self-imposed panic sets in again. This is the alarm you feel when you realize that now you have to maintain and <u>exceed</u> what you just accomplished; because there's no coasting in life, not in your business, not in intimate relationships, physical health, or any area.

Even if you accomplish whatever you set out to do, you are unknowingly and immediately setting yourself up for a hamster wheel rat race needing to exceed it. That's exhausting and anxiety-inducing. **And even if you do**

achieve what you've set out to do, you end up at the bottom of another mountain needing to climb even higher.

Downtime is not a concept that exists for most achievers. Worse, even while achieving goals, it's never fulfilling long-term. More often than not, you are striving to accomplish what your parents, friends, or society thinks you *should* be doing. It is not what you truly want, so you feel like you're attempting to push forward by going against the grain of your true passion. That is no way to live.

This mentality often consumes the highest achievers. Conversely, those who are not prone to achievement often feel stuck, like failures or feel like they are not good enough. I want to save you from a lifetime of these feelings.

No 90-day action plan, mentorship, or coaching will make any difference if you don't believe you deserve the goal you have set for yourself. Self-sabotage will reliably occur throughout your process resulting in intense frustration and stress, eventually leading to burnout, which means you sometimes quit the effort altogether.

Self Development Courses and Books

I've been a lifelong student of self-development courses, books, mentors, seminars, all leading me to spending hours of daily work on myself. I couldn't calculate how much time and how many thousands of dollars I've spent learning from the best of the best. All this personal development work has lead me to creating online courses of my own while also hosting live seminars that benefit people worldwide.

While I most often get great feedback on my programs, I often don't feel satisfied with many of the courses I have taken. I often ask myself, what's the essence of an online course or book? It's the author sifting through research and experience and presenting the best material available.

However, there is no personal interaction possible with a book or an online program. You are consuming the material through your already ingrained deserving belief. So, you can be handed the keys to the kingdom on how to get what you want, but if you have an undeserving belief in that area, you fall into one of these traps:

- You don't believe what the author says is possible
  (So you don't apply it).
- You believe it, but don't act on it (Procrastination).
- You act on it but unknowingly self-sabotage your process along the way.

No matter how great the material you're given, if it's being interpreted through an undeserving belief you will not produce the results others have achieved. Books and courses cannot interact with you to flip your switch from undeserving to deserving. You're in complete control when you open a book or go through a course; so how much you consume and digest (and what you choose to act on and apply) is entirely up to you.

That is why books and self-learning courses can be limited in value. A great example are the spiritual texts read daily throughout the world by millions. These books contain incredible wisdom on how to live a healthy, happy life and how to become a constructive member of society. With all of this wisdom available, how many people are actually applying it to make a real tangible difference in their lives and communities? I would say that it's a small percentage. **I'm not discrediting the quality of the wisdom of the texts; I'm discrediting the medium of transfer to the recipient.**

I'm well aware that the very same thing can happen with this book. My utmost goal is that at least one principle I write will inspire you to use The Deserving Process to regain or create your deserving belief. Knowing the power of your deserving belief will not change your life. Doing The Deserving Process will. I share The Deserving Process with you in chapter 5. If you do it repeatedly, within a short time you will start seeing your life change, feeling better in the moment, and having more optimism about your future.

Mentoring/Coaching

I'm ever grateful for the numerous coaches and mentors I've had, from my early youth sports days to investing well over six figures and traveling across the world for my own personal and business development. One of my mentors, Robert Gibson, has stuck by my side through thick and thin. In our weekly calls every Tuesday night he offers incredibly tough love and unconditional support. He also provides his guidance via text messages and email. I would not be where I am today without his wisdom, guidance, and tireless help.

Robert was, in fact, the biggest influence in my decision to create coaching programs of my own, paving the way for me to do it with his non-stop support. So for everyone for whom I've made a difference, some credit goes to Robert. He showed me what was possible in my life by not putting up with my excuses or stubbornness and he was *always* there when needed.

As wise as Robert is, there are numerous times he will lay out a perfect plan for me to follow and then he hears silence on my end. Or, he hears "Yes" over and over, but I don't do what he says. My not taking action is not because his plan did not make sense. It is because I don't believe I deserve what his plan will produce. So, I procrastinate and defend my excuses. This drives Robert nuts, especially because I invariably end up flipping my switch and taking the self-deserving action, but not directly because of Robert's advice.

Even with a great coach, mentor, or therapist, you are interpreting everything they tell you through your deserving belief filter. You're choosing what to believe, what actions to do, where to procrastinate, and where to give excuses. Unless the mentor is focusing on flipping your switch your time together is not going to result in advancing you to what you want. And, if you do get what you're after, self-sabotage will ultimately cause you to lose it.

Most importantly, no one knows the exact steps you need to take to reach your goal. No one has walked in your shoes, experienced your upbringing, or your relationships. No one inherently knows the exact steps for you to take. Only you know what those steps are when your mind is clear and inspired to reveal them to you.

Meditation and Visualization

I respect and endorse all forms of meditation and have happily used many variations over the past ten years, including the use of transcendental meditation, breathwork, visualization, body awareness, you name it. All have value in distinct ways, each allowing you to reduce physical and emotional stress, while producing more ease, awareness, and mindfulness.

However, if you intend to create something new in your life, like a relationship or income level, meditation rarely makes the difference. These practices were not created to change your deserving belief. So yes, meditation is highly valuable but won't flip your switch from undeserving to deserving.

* * * * *

No matter how great the self-help material or mentor may be, we now see that none of those methods work when you harbor stubborn undeserving beliefs. The opposite is true as well. As soon as you flip your switch to deserving, you'll end up with a newfound commitment to getting what you are after. Your purpose and determination become dramatically stronger. You will meet the people who are meant to positively influence your journey. And, most magical of all is that life's synchronicities and serendipities fall into place for you. The timing and rhythm of events will all just flow. All of this adds to more happiness, joy, and peace of mind—even before you get what you are after.

That's what you can expect to experience from using The Deserving Process. And, that's what you're going to learn in this book.

* * * * *

Most Important Chapter 2 Takeaways

- Every rationale that explains why your life isn't working can be traced back to your belief that you simply do not deserve it.
- Traditional goal setting can be very dangerous. It often leads to unfulfillment, unhappiness, stress, and anxiety. Have goals, but don't get stuck in the constant and neverending goal setting trap of life.
- No program, teacher, book, or seminar is going be effective unless your belief system is flipped from undeserving to deserving. No matter how educational or beneficial the learning or growth tool is, you will not fully absorb or implement it with an undeserving belief.

End of Chapter 2: BONUS RESOURCES

If you feel stuck with your current goal setting approach: Do any of these sound like you?
- You accomplish most goals, but just as quickly you feel the need to set yet another goal. Even if you are successful and have accomplished what you set out to do, you're constantly doubting your achievements.
- Your common theme is starting a goal feeling inspired but losing momentum and quitting along your path toward it.
- Your entire process of achieving your goals feels like you're constantly pushing and going against the grain, exhausted, stressed, and burnt out.

I will show you how you can still have goals without the incessant pressure, anxiety, or frustration that has come from traditional goal setting in the past.

Do you feel stuck in your meditation or visualization practice? Have you gone through self-help book after self-help book and not seen the personal change promised? Are you working with a coach and not experiencing the growth you had hoped for or anticipated?

There's a reason that good intentions and going through the motions on proven programs are not enough. I go through each example of self-development and show where you're not seeing the breakthrough, and why.

Chapter 2

Workbook for Deservingness

Write down your answers: Which areas of your life feel like a never-ending cycle of goal setting—without ever getting a lasting positive outcome or enjoying the process of reaching your goal?

Areas to Consider:
- Diet/Weight/Body
- Financial
- Relationships/Family/Love
- Peace of Mind/Happiness
- Career

In which part of your life are you most focused and is most important?
- Why are you setting these goals?
- Who will they benefit and why?
- How many years have you been stuck in this goal-setting cycle?
- How does it feel? How would it feel if your goals were different (and successful)?

Chapter 3

The Endless Chain Reaction of Your Pain

One of my favorite clients is Allen. Before we began working together, he'd been involved in self-growth work for years and had developed a strong mental attitude that contributed to his being a great husband, father, friend, and entrepreneur. When we began he had already been very successful in business for 30 years. However, he was feeling burnt out, "crispy around the edges" as he described it. He also calculated he had spent over $200,000 throughout his life on personal and professional development!

His personal discipline is impressive. He wakes up each day at 4:30 a.m. to begin his morning routine in order to create a sharp focus for the day. So by the time he gets to the office, he's already done a full workout.

Allen attended a live seminar of mine where he learned how to flip his switch from undeserving to deserving. A few months later he sent me a video from his tree-lined backyard in New England. In it, as he talked about the progress he'd made, he was glowing and felt great, savoring the beautiful spring day, complete with birds chirping behind him.

The previous month he made $25,000 more than his normal income, without working any more hours. It happened so easily he was shocked and had his staff re-check the numbers multiple times. They were correct. Since then, instead of feeling burnt out, he has reported being more inspired than ever, going in each morning with happy anticipation.

You may be thinking right now, I'm not a doctor or successful business owner... *how does this relate to me?* You're completely right. Many of the examples given are from clients I work with personally. However, deserving beliefs apply to everyone, even if you do not own a business or have dramatically different circumstances than the professionals detailed thus far. You could be a single mother, retired grandfather, or teenager navigating adolescence and apply The Deserving Process in your life.

Allen brings up a powerful point here. **Believing you deserve what you want doesn't just come after you get it.** Using The Deserving Process to flip your switch before it's present in your life is the ideal way to create and attract what you want. This applies equally in business or your personal finances, love life, self-image, peace of mind or any area of life you choose.

Your level of deservedness is **not** consistent across all areas of life. For example, you might take great care of your body, believing you deserve to be in good health. Yet you might neglect your financial health causing it to be in disarray. Perhaps your finances are more affected by beliefs about not deserving abundance. In other words, feeling deserving does not encompass your beliefs as a whole. There are areas in your life that you have the belief in and areas that you do not, all with differing levels of 'deserving' strength.

At this point, you should know it is unlikely your deserving beliefs are going to change all on their own. So if you do not alter them, you are setting yourself up for unchanging results in those areas of your life. Next, you will see how undeserving can sabotage you unless you become aware of exactly where it is happening.

* * * * *

Finances and Wealth

My paternal grandfather, Grandpa Dan, never let go of his Marine Corps code of discipline, even when he was with his grandchildren. In fact, his military demeanor seemed to intensify around my brother and me. One family vacation morning as we waited impatiently to go to the beach, my brother Adam and I were fooling around tossing a tennis ball against the hotel hallway walls, a bit too loudly.

The manager complained, and Grandpa Dan was livid. In fact, he got so upset that—in advance of the beach—he made us come with him on an errand, a trip to the bank. On the entire way down the street, Grandpa Dan told us that we had to march like soldiers, right there in public.

Inside the bank, we were forced to stand in silence facing one of the circular pillars one inch from our face while everyone inside stared at us in bewilderment. Then we marched back to the hotel. I was so shaken up by all this. And I can still remember Grandpa Dan's face flushed red, his forehead lines appearing as his anger built and the screaming began.

I'll never forget another occasion when, at age six, he took me out to lunch. We finished eating, and he was adding in the tip and his signature on the check. Even though I was scared of him, I looked up to him, tall, intense, and imposing as ever.

I leaned over his arm with genuine curiosity to see what his signature looked like. What I didn't anticipate was his assumption that I was actually looking at how much tip he was leaving the waitress! The fit of screaming I was subjected to left the entire restaurant silent.

For most of us, the most negatively ingrained emotional area of our life is money. Everyone has a level of anxiety, fear, or a sense of undeserving in the realm of personal finances and wealth, even the rich. Whether you are just getting by financially or are a multimillionaire, there's no escaping the emotional stress money can so easily cause in your life. **No matter how much money people amass, they still often feel the same anxieties and stress as when they had much less.**

Stressful financial thoughts become incessant worries: Will I have enough to pay my bills at the end of the month? Will I ever be able to retire? Will I be able to make or save enough to give my children the experiences I want them to have?

These questions don't merely disappear if and when money is no longer an issue for you. Those concerns often turn into anxiety and fear of losing the wealth that's been made, or of mismanaging it, and most peculiarly, *still thinking you do not have enough.* So wherever you are on the financial spectrum, you could likely use a greater deserving belief about money.

Here is how an undeserving belief commonly plays out in your financial world:

You've never been able to commit to a budget, control your spending, or properly allocate your money to eliminate debt, save, and take care of your needs and those who count on you. This is a basic symptom of self-sabotage, not believing you deserve financial freedom. And if you don't believe you deserve it, why would you display the basic discipline of saving, budgeting, knowing your numbers, and paying off debts? You wouldn't.

Another example is unnecessary emotional spending—retail therapy. Feeling entitled to buying a new wardrobe or expensive jewelry is often motivated by the desire to escape current stresses. And it winds up being financial self-sabotage. This is not a wise personal expenditure and further keeps you stuck in the financial hamster wheel.

Or, conversely, you might be a diligent saver, very frugal and conscious of where your money is spent. Yet it feels as if you're in the financial hamster wheel, running in circles year after year, getting nowhere. Why? Because your expenses continually rise as your income does. Or perhaps unforeseen accidents occur that drain your savings.

And no matter what you do (even though you are doing all you know to do) you can't seem to break this cycle of feeling financially stuck. Saving for the home down payment, getting approved for a mortgage or being able to finance the desired car always seems to be just out of your reach and control.

Financial undeserving shows up in the wealthy too. How many people have all the money in the world and still don't know how to enjoy their lives? Remember: Unhealthy and destructive emotions don't disappear based on your increased financial circumstances. Instead, they intensify. **Unhealthy emotions and undeserving beliefs only change depending upon how effectively you have dealt with them directly.**

So if you have unhealthy beliefs around deserving money, even if you come into great wealth (inheritance, a financial windfall) you still have those original negative emotions. Studies of lottery winners reveal that, on average, they are in a worse financial condition within seven years of winning the lottery than before they won.

Why? Because the same emotions and mentalities that were present their entire life (forcing them to purchase lottery tickets because they did not believe they had enough money, or couldn't make money on their own) didn't change after they won. So, the same beliefs produced the results in their life of not having enough money or not being able to make it on their own.

The lethal fear of financial insecurity can even lead to incredibly wealthy individuals committing suicide, a shocking act that causes disbelief to many. "But he/she had everything?" they lament. The last scene of the movie *All the Money In the World* shows the wealthiest man on Earth at the time, J. Paul Getty, all alone in his home clutching an expensive painting he had to pry off his wall the last minutes of his life. Meanwhile, sounds of alarms and flashing lights in the middle of the night blare during his last moments alive. It's a tragic, haunting scene. So having astronomical wealth does not protect you from incredible fear, doubt, insecurity, and jealousy. All these negative emotions lead to self-sabotage and intense unhappiness.

A very successful doctor attended one of my live seminars because he was frustrated, feeling 'stuck' at his income level (even though it was a very high income). While working together, he looked back on his upbringing and realized that his conditioned deserving belief was to do better than his father had done financially. Once he achieved that, which he already had, he never had created a new belief about what he truly deserved financially. So he stayed stuck and stressed at that same income level.

It's not worth it to endure a lifetime of anxiety, agony, or stress over your financial situation. Do the work to flip your switch and gain not only financial independence, but freedom from anxiety, fear, and money-related stress. **When you create peace of mind around money and the ability to increase your wealth,** *you've got the best of both worlds.*

* * * * *

Romance and Relationships

All through childhood I remember hearing my father pleading with my mother to get a job to supplement the family income. From years of that conditioning and their subsequent separation and divorce, I made a strong mental connection between financial deprivation and romantic relationships: If finances don't work out, *neither does the relationship.*

This assumption first showed up when I finished graduate school and was responsible for earning a full-time income. There existed no student loan for real life! So how was I ever going to pay off almost $200,000 in student loans?! Making it even more insurmountable, I was living in the most expensive neighborhood in the most expensive city in the world. I became very conscious of my income and the lifestyle it would provide me in the future.

Before that point, I usually had a girlfriend, and I can tell you that the financial aspect of our relationship rarely entered my mind. I wasn't concerned about her salary or job, or how much money her parents had. However, once I was on my own financially and professional stress set in, my financial belief system reverted to what it had been when I was a child.

Fear and anxiety set in and I started to become very conscious of whom I dated. Why? I didn't want the relationship to be a financial strain on me. Because of this belief, any woman I was going to choose to spend my life with had better have her financial life together so it wouldn't lead to our relationship destructing. It's no surprise that every one of my next few girlfriends was very financially independent, most often from impressive business savvy and very high income.

It wasn't that I was seeking them out consciously, but it happened without me even realizing or intending it due to my strong subconscious belief. I likely passed up many great potential partners due to this blind spot. And I stayed longer with girlfriends who had the financial independence I desired even though the relationship wasn't working.

When I became aware of this and applied The Deserving Process, I was able to let that mentality surrounding my relationships go. My priorities instead evolved to different criteria. I wanted a partner with great character, someone who was loving, a true match. So regardless of a woman's financial situation, I was now open to getting to know her based on our compatibility and character, not on her financial stability.

Quickly review your past romantic long-term relationships or the one you are in now. When you focus on honestly observing your history, are there common themes of why each began, progressed, or ended? For instance, if your top priority is finding an amazingly loving life partner for companionship, perhaps procrastination and self-sabotage could show up as:

- You don't put yourself out there or let people know you're available.
- You turn down date requests without genuine reason.
- You only go on dates with those who are not your ideal vision in a partner (self-sabotage through avoidance).

Undeserving beliefs appear at every phase of your relationships. Yours may set in when your connection turns exclusive. Looking over your relationship history, you might observe that most of your intimate connections last from six to twelve months and always end similarly. Perhaps, he or she always "changed" after the six-month initial honeymoon phase. Whatever is showing up in your dating history, there's likely a common theme if connection and fulfillment are lacking.

If you're currently in a long-term committed relationship it may feel like:

- Your relationship is stale, boring or even abusive, but you feel too stuck to leave because of children, finances, or fear of being on your own and disrupting the status quo.
- Your relationship is unbalanced, and you feel undervalued, unacknowledged, or even invisible.
- You are now in a completely different phase of your life—enduring the loss of a spouse and not knowing if romance is still possible for you or if

you should seek it.

No matter your age or relationship status, the inherent notion so many people have of feeling unlovable and lonely with no foreseeable change in the future is far too common.

I imagine you can see some of these themes *clearly* in the lives of your best friends who somehow never stop complaining about *their* romantic drama. It is far easier to see what is obviously defective in other people's relationships. You likely want to shake your distraught friend and say, *"Why do you keep dating people who treat you like trash!?"* or *"Why do you constantly get involved with unavailable men?"*

Your real power, however, is being able to look at *your* romantic history and see the themes present. It is not worth wasting the rest of your years repeating the same unfulfilling love and relationship patterns.

The married people I coach often apply the same listening strategies with their spouse as they do with their clients. And I'm always delighted to receive a text from a private client who reports on progress at home! Suddenly, they choose to change their conditioned way of responding to their spouse, and instead, show they truly listened.

The most common reply from their spouse is a very happy and sarcastic "Thank you for finally hearing me... and what did you do with my husband?!"

* * * * *

Self-Image

We live in a very judgmental society. A billboard in Manhattan reads: "New York City: Where you're judged more for your shoes than your religion or sexual orientation."

I used to be insecure walking into expensive fashionable clothing stores in attempts to upgrade my wardrobe. I was afraid the salespeople would judge me for the attire I walked in with and therefore not take me seriously. Just the thought of an odd stare kept me from even entering exclusive shops. For years—due to this insecurity—I simply avoided them.

Unfortunately, this painful lack of confidence is a concern for many people. It is like standing paralyzed with your lunch tray in hand on the first day of middle school, praying someone you know will wave you over to sit with them. But, looking at the sea of faces it doesn't happen, and you feel everyone is staring at you, judging where you choose to sit. However, now it's 30, 40, 50 years later, yet you feel the same angst in social situations.

With the new norm of social media bombarding us with everyone else's life adventures—social anxiety is increasing exponentially.

Younger generations with access to smartphones spend hours losing themselves in others' lives. And slowly but surely, social and body anxiety are being planted as people compare themselves to—even photoshopped—others.

Social media is just one avenue of self-inflicted compare and despair. Comparison and judgment are inherent in all humans. It's not going to stop, and I'm not going to try to get you to stop comparing yourself to others. **The real dilemma is not that we judge others,** *it's that we constantly perceive others are judging us.*

Instead of trying to stop judging and assessing others, how can we stop being affected by believing others are judging us? For females, this happens most with body and image. For males, it's success and accomplishment.

Since we can't stop others from judging, we can shift how we feel about ourselves when it's happening. This is where your deserving belief counts. If you believe you are deserving of respect and admiration, that's how you will see yourself in the mirror and feel about yourself in public no matter who is looking at you.

No matter how beautiful or well-dressed a woman is, if she does not feel great about how she looks, she will not appear as attractive to others. Not feeling good about yourself shows up in your body posture, facial expression, and the invisible energy you unknowingly radiate. These subtle changes in your energy speak volumes to your observers—more than your body shape, makeup, or great outfit.

You can start decreasing and eliminating these feelings through daily work in believing you're deserving of looking and feeling great and receiving positive attention and respect.

Important to note is body weight and self-image are completely separate issues. A higher body weight than "average" does not mean a lower self-image comes attached. When you have the deserving belief, you learn to value yourself for all of your qualities and not compartmentalize yourself.

An enlightening moment for me was during my first year in practice when Rose came in as a new patient for chronic pain. She was overweight, clinically obese by objective standards. I asked her if she was interested in addressing weight loss as well as the pain, which was not directly related. She confidently and quickly replied not at all. She loved her body just how it was.

I later came to learn she was a successful plus-size fashion blogger. Her confidence and self-worth impressed me immensely and I saw her as she saw herself, one of the most beautiful and well-dressed women I have ever met.

* * * * *

Body Weight and Size

One of the biggest industries is weight loss and always will be. If there really was a single magic solution that worked the issue would be solved for hundreds of millions of people who are constantly jumping from diet to diet. Countless diets claim to have finally discovered the missing ingredient for your quick and permanent weight loss. And, even though all the commercial testimonials are likely from real people who have lost and kept off the weight, we know countless others who have tried the diet, followed it exactly as prescribed, and have not reached their goals.

If weight loss is your goal I'm sure you have tried many approaches. Some diets you've stuck with and some you quit because it was difficult and your willpower gave out. With some diets, you didn't see changes quickly enough or your undeserving self-sabotage kicked in (in the way it always does for you around food, exercise, and weight loss intentions).

All diets benefit and fail participants. It's clear the determinant for achieving the desired results is not the diet itself, but rather, the person *on* the diet. **The single underlying factor determining whether the diet will work is whether the dieter believes he or she is deserving of the results they are after.**

The dieter may believe in the method of the diet (after all, they likely wouldn't begin with it if they did not) *but NOT believe deserving to lose the weight*. This is the real issue. If you've been jumping from diet to diet, workout to workout, and either quitting, self-sabotaging, or laboring away without getting the results you want, what should you do?

Before you begin your next attempt, you need to flip your switch in this area because the real reason it's not working is because you do not believe you deserve the results you are after. And that's not your fault. Remember, this is not conscious. Your undeserving beliefs were planted in you from incidents or experiences from your past. We will explore this in more detail in the next chapter.

* * * * *

Health and Healing

While sharing the premise of this book with a small group I met at a retreat center during the initial writing process, Rodney, a very thoughtful and contemplative retreat house manager, said to me, " the concept ofyour book you told us about at dinner was on my mind all night. And, I was wondering if the deserving belief applies to the healing process as well?" If Rodney had not asked that question, it might have been inadvertently excluded from the book.

You've likely heard of the incredible power of the placebo effect. This is when a patient believes a treatment is healing them when in fact, the treatment holds no medicinal efficacy. The medicine is most often delivered in the form of a sugar pill though the patient is informed it is the medication for their ailment. The placebo effect doesn't have anything to do with deserving, but it proves the power of belief in the realm of our health and healing.[1]

The Placebo Effect is such a significant concept that there are countless case studies of patients being surgically operated on the wrong limb and having full recovery purely because they thought their operation was done correctly. No physiological science can justify this other than our mind's ability and power to influence our body's healing when we truly believe it should.

So how does the deserving belief tie into your healing process? Do you know more than one person who has the same medical condition and has tried the same remedies or procedures and gotten different results? Absolutely.

Whether it's treatment for acne or cancer, that is how healing works. Everyone's history, genetics, lifestyle, and deserving-healing belief are unique, causing tremendous variability in patient response. I'm not saying the only difference is the patient's deserving belief, however, it is a vital part of the process. If a patient does not believe they deserve to heal, it will make a significant negative impact on their healing process.

Many health concerns also arise from an undeserving belief. Here's one way this happens: When we have strong undeserving in a significant area of our life it will cause a tremendous amount of mental stress (financial insecurity for example). Chronic stress impairs our immune system, leaving us weaker to fight off outside invaders whether bacteria, viruses, or a host of other pathogens that can easily enter the body or manifest from within.[2] If these intruders overpower your immune response a condition develops that you are now forced to deal with.

And, again, I must reiterate that this concept should not be taken out of context: An undeserving belief in our health can negatively affect our ability to stay healthy and affect our healing process. This does not mean that every health issue or lack of healing is only stemming from an undeserving belief.

Understanding this, if you have experienced difficulty healing a condition, before moving on to yet another potentially costly procedure or to taking a drug with potentially negative side effects, you should address any undeserving beliefs present that could be hindering your healing in addition to what is recommended by your doctor.

Additionally, we are all at a point on the deserving spectrum for overall health. We all have a *personal health set-point.* As always, it is a subconscious belief about what we *believe* we deserve to have. For example, we all have financial set-points that relate to our income level and wealth. When you change your deserving belief, you can change your subconscious set-point.

We all know people who seem to have great energy and body weight who all eat differently, exercise differently, and have completely different lifestyles. So, what is the distinguishing factor when one is caught off guard and comes down with serious illness? Once again, it's your deserving belief set-point for your health.

This plays out in your life without you consciously thinking about it. Your lifestyle is a display in support of your belief. For example, you won't eat fast food often, drink alcohol in excess, smoke, compromise your sleep on a routine basis, or constantly dwell in negativity. These poor choices would not make any sense to someone who believes they deserve to have health as a normal lifelong state of being.

However, if you have an undeserving belief in your health, you are far more likely not to take your lifestyle as seriously. If you're under the assumption you have no control over your weight and never will, then why not indulge in your favorite sweets, bad fats, and fried foods whenever you wish? Not doing so isn't going to change anything anyway, right? You're in a state of both helplessness and hopelessness.

Expanding on this subject, beyond your lifestyle habits, your thoughts and emotions control the release of countless hormones responsible for metabolic regulation, fat-burning and body physiology that keep you in or out of shape. These play just as important a role, if not more, in the overall health, aging, and healing of your body.

What should you take from this? It doesn't matter if you have an illness or diagnosis you can't resolve right now or not. Your deserving belief in the realm of your health is operating at all times. If you don't have the general levels of energy and physical health you aspire to, it's time to address it. Life is too precious to go through in chronic pain, fatique, or not feeling your best throughout your day.

You WILL change your lifestyle habits when you flip your switch for deserving full health. Thereafter, your life will be a positive affirmation and demonstration of your inner state. Not least important, your family and loved ones will be grateful you chose your health too.

* * * * *

Happiness and Peace of Mind

All the money, possessions, and popularity cannot provide you happiness or peace of mind in the long-term. Even in the short-term, it is often fleeting. And, it doesn't mean there's anything wrong with them; they just don't provide lasting happiness or true peace of mind on their own.

What does endure is how you feel on a day-to-day basis, no matter if you've achieved your material goals or not. So whether you are in the middle of a breakdown or major stress, you're able to maintain a stable mood, a happiness and peace of mind set-point.

Many professionals I have worked with are in some kind of a life transition, some forced to relocate for family reasons. Mark was moving his family back to Eastern Europe from the United States because he wanted to be closer to his relatives and raise his children in the same culture he had known as a boy. When we began, he was extremely stressed because he felt pressured to build his practice as quickly as possible in order to sell it at the best price. After a few months, he wrote me to say that working together had given him the result he wanted: peace of mind for his future and for his family to return home.

If you grew up in an environment that fostered happiness, where a peaceful household was normal and expected, you lucked out. Most of us did not. We saw our parents struggle in many ways. Sometimes they would lose their patience, cry, get angry or maybe even scream and fight. It set an expectation, a deserving belief that struggle and strife were the patterns to follow. It's how life is supposed to be.

I used to be an angry kind of person. Add alcohol to the mix, and it was like putting gasoline on a flame. During my college years at NYU, I first began to observe how my emotions and state of mind affected my behavior. This new level of self-awareness was very revealing and healing to me. I now understood that it did not make sense to be angry. And, I knew that I didn't want my life to be dominated by this emotion.

John Barna, an NYU professor of classics said to me, **"Anger takes up a lot of energy."** Once we got to know one another, Dr. Barna wrote a five page hand-written letter of recommendation on my behalf for graduate school. When I called the admissions office to confirm they had received my full application, the woman exclaimed that she had never seen a letter of recommendation quite like that one! I still have a copy of it today. Thank you, John.

The wise lessons I learned from John really sunk in during my undergraduate years and an unforgettable vision started appearing in my head: It's a beautiful, clear, sunny weekend morning in the New York countryside, close to where I grew up. A middle-aged male—resembling me—is driving a gorgeous blue convertible down a hilly straightaway country road, one that cuts through a member-only golf course. On each side of the road are perfectly manicured rolling lawns.

He is feeling a total sense of freedom, relaxed and happy, dressed in a light blue linen button-down shirt with sleeves casually rolled up to the elbows. As he listens to the music he loves, he's cruising down that road with the wind blowing through his hair, feeling carefree, smiling at the simple pleasures of driving on a beautiful day.

Then he stops for gas, leans on his car as the tank fills up, still feeling a calm, joyful demeanor, total peace of mind. I got the sense he was very successful, kind, optimistic, and open. Whatever problems he might have don't seem to weigh heavily on his conscience. He is the kind of person who deals with his issues rather than be consumed or stressed by them, or avoiding them altogether. He is a responsible man with a loving family. So on this day, maybe he is out on this solo joyride, picking up lunch for everyone at home.

For years, I kept seeing this vision of someone else, someone older than me whom I did not know, but respected. He was someone I idealized and admired, the person I aspired to *be*. But, I knew it wasn't the car or clothing that would turn me into him. Instead, it was his emotional calm, his mindset and beliefs that were creating the person I saw.

Years later, I found myself experiencing the same sense of calm as he did. I was in the car on a relaxing drive cutting through a golf course, wearing similar clothes, and most importantly, feeling happiness and total peace of mind. It didn't happen overnight or with the purchase of a car. But it did happen.

I admit that when I first saw this vision, I was harboring much anger inside. However, I flipped my switch, and in time, the anger faded, and so with it the way I used to look at life. In my day-to-day routine, I now felt dramatically different. If I had not done the work to transform my thinking from undeserving to deserving, my life would have continued as in angry default. I would have made good money; I'm sure of that. I would have had possessions and cars and friends and a family. But, the anger wouldn't have changed.

As the old wives' tale says, time heals all wounds, sadness and anger and disappointment gradually fade away. **But, in fact, time does *not* heal. It buries. It suffocates**. **It creates a hard shell around issues we don't want to deal with**. And with each passing year, that outer shell makes it tougher to ever heal that inner wound.

In short, we all have beliefs about the level of happiness we deserve. The same is true of your peace of mind. If your current level of either emotional state is not where you want it to be, you can change that. You are not stuck with it forever.

* * * * *

Two Significant Ways Your Undeserving Belief Can Show Up

1. Denial

If you're reading this book, then you're not in complete denial! However, we all have some level of denial about our mindset and how profoundly it's affecting our happiness. Technically, denial is a coping skill. We learn to deny as children to help us process traumatic events. Then as we age, it becomes distorted in a fixed way of being and thinking, like a habit. A bad one.

Recently, I admitted my cardiovascular health was awful. I knew if I had to run just one lap around a track I would be hunched over sucking wind by the end of it, if I even made it to the finish line. Clearly, after the majority of my organized sports career ended in high school, I had become lazy and gotten away without doing any cardiovascular activity. I was, however, able to disguise this little secret behind the facade of how my body looked externally, relatively fit without exercise.

But today I have a true deserving belief when it comes to my health and well-being. I've always viewed myself as healthy. It's a core belief that motivates me to live in a way that perpetuates good health. So, after a while of knowing my cardio health was poor, I had to do something about it and challenged myself to start running (okay, jogging).

I discovered the app "Couch to 5K" and believed I could complete the challenge. So for the next 90 days, three times a week, I didn't miss one run. And as I expanded my stamina, I was eventually able to jog five kilometers in 20 minutes without stopping. I was really proud of myself for sticking with it, accomplishing the goal I set for myself. And of course, I immediately felt a lot better in the day after the runs. Do I enjoy running now? Still no. But I'm very glad I did it.

So why did I choose to challenge myself to an activity I detest instead of quitting along the way? Because I have an inherent *deserving* belief in my overall health. Armed with that, I was able to overcome my short-term denial that had led to my poor cardio condition. However, if you don't have a deserving belief in the area of your denial it will most likely stay with you for life. And that's exactly what we are going to interrupt by flipping your switch.

2. Self-Sabotage

Whether or not the five major life areas discussed previously are what you're seeking to improve or not, self-sabotage will affect you until it is addressed. Here is an example of how it plays out in countless people's lives today. See if you can relate to any of Jane's day:

She wakes up to an alarm blaring, still tired and now running late to work. She's hurried and stressed and doesn't even stop to eat a healthy breakfast, too rushed to bother. Forget about a morning workout. From the start of her day she is consumed with negativity about her upcoming work responsibilities, getting increasingly stressed as she scans all the texts and emails from colleagues about looming deadlines.

To escape the pressure before work, she jumps on Facebook and Instagram, which provides some entertaining distraction on her commute. In the news feeds, she sees all the happy people she knows posting about their perfect weekends (as well as targeted ads catered to her most private questions and concerns she googled within the last 90 days).

She compares herself to each of her social media friends and the result is a recurrence of her anxiety and low self-esteem, never feeling good enough in comparison to others. Haunting her is the FOMO (fear of missing out), missing the best of what everybody else is doing with their lives.

Then she gets to work and puts on a smile to satisfy peers and management, more concerned about not making any mistakes than about performing her best. Social media breaks are consistent as her inbox and to-do list gets exponentially larger every day.

She gets home exhausted and opens a bottle of red wine and the newest low-calorie pint of ice cream to watch her favorite reality TV series. Although she is trying to lose ten pounds before the wedding she is in next month, she needs *something* to escape the stress of the workday.

She convinces herself that this low-cal ice cream with a skinny cow on the front can't be *that bad*. Vegging out to her reality series and wasting time puts her into further anxiety and undeserving states, along with the horrid feelings of scrolling through her dating apps and prospects that look less than appealing. She eventually falls asleep without brushing her teeth and forgetting to return her parents' earlier text needing to speak.

Jane wakes up the next morning to do this day all over again, still tired and feeling stuck. The only hope she feels is the anticipation of a few upcoming weekend social events and escape from the monotony of her workdays. Her real-life social connections put her face to face with the same anxieties she felt in social media, but her discomfort is even more intensified because there's no *sign off button* in real life. Instead of being able to be the silent, secret observer behind a screen, she feels others are judging her fashion style, hair, summer plans, and single status.

Days turn into weeks, to months, to years, and this pattern of self-abuse becomes the normal way of life. Jane wonders how her existence has turned into this weekly cycle. Her self-esteem is flawed, her work doesn't inspire her, her health is compromised, and she has little romance to comfort her. Overall, her life is lacking real joy and peace of mind.

Jane is trapped, a victim of her own behavior patterns and subconscious belief that she is not deserving of a better life. It's all on autopilot, and she doesn't realize there is a way out, a solution to her despondency. How could anything change unless she wins the lottery or prince charming sweeps her off her feet?

Jane's true self-sabotage is not the eating of ice cream or the binging on social media. It's that she feels she is hopelessly stuck with no way out. What no one has ever told her is that she is NOT stuck. She is not trapped in this life with no options. Using The Deserving Process daily, she will not only start to feel better about herself and her situation, she will also choose to make changes that don't feel burdensome, overwhelming, or undoable. And day-by-day, each area of her life will begin to change for the better.

Chapter 3 Most Important Takeaways

- Undeserving beliefs manifest themselves differently for everyone, in all areas of life, from finances and romance to your health and career choices.
- You can be sure that if you experience self-sabotage or denial, no doubt your undeserving beliefs, like hidden puppeteers, are pulling your strings.
- To most easily locate where your undeserving beliefs are affecting you, take an honest inventory of every area of your life that *isn't* how you want it to be.

End of Chapter 3: BONUSES

In my own career, I flipped my switch from feeling fearful to bold, taking command of my future. You can do it too. I'll share what made the biggest difference for me professionally and how you can apply it too.

Learn the simple, yet profound, communication technique I teach clients that combats the self-sabotage and denial that too easily manifests itself in our relationships. It will dramatically strengthen your bond with your spouse and children, close friends or colleagues and anywhere communication is most important in your life.

Has social media consumption become a distracting self-sabotage? It's okay. I've been there too. That's why I've added a list of simple tips and tricks to control the amount of time you spend on social media without feeling like you're depriving yourself.

Chapter 4

Meet The People Controlling Your Life

I'm out in New York City celebrating at dinner with my good friend Jayson. Why? He just sold a piece of his company to a private equity firm for a huge sum. After all his years of business success, including taking his first company public, this was his biggest financial windfall ever.

As he told me, when he started out professionally he was just a salesman, frequently on the road prospecting for clients, doing anything he could to drum up business. After a few years he figured he didn't need to be the middleman anymore and could sell the same products and make a lot more. So he created his own company selling the same product. And he's been super successful ever since.

Jayson embodied the inherent belief he *deserved* to make more than he did as a salesman. Growing up, his mother and father always believed in him, even more than he believed in himself. At our dinner he shared he was going to the cemetery to leave flowers for his parents who had died 20 years earlier. I asked if he customarily went to their graves each year. He replied, "No, I've never done it. But this time, with the good fortune of the latest business success, I want to thank and acknowledge them for always believing in me."

That night I shared with him the deserving belief concept as the ultimate determinant in getting what you want. He listened without interrupting, paused, reflected and said " that's absolutely right. And I've never thought of it that way. I've always just had an inherent belief I deserved abundance. Maybe that's why I've never been much of a saver of money throughout my life.

"Why? I've always believed I'll have enough and there's more where that came from. I just believed I deserved it, so I never held back on treating myself and enjoying life to the fullest. And that caused me never to give up on any goal, even when times were really tough. I grew up in Queens without a silver spoon in my mouth. I still remember the neighbors who gave us quarters instead of one cent candies on Halloween. My friends and I always appreciated their generosity. All these years later I still remember those neighbors."

Unlike the majority of us, Jayson was fortunate to believe that he was deserving of financial abundance. Indeed, most who have the life they want don't ever consciously flip their switch. Their emotional compass is set from the start from as early as they can remember. And in Jayson's case, it all began with deeply supportive parents.

Unfortunately, we're not all as fortunate as Jayson, blessed with parents who believed in our talents and unique aptitudes. So few of us have deserving beliefs naturally "turned on" by our parents. In fact, negative events throughout our childhood actually flip our switches *off*. Growing up is tough.

Our parents are not given instruction manuals about how to instill positive self-regard. Teachers, caregivers, and authority figures make mistakes all the time, projecting their own fears and insecurities and judgments onto children. They can say words that shatter a child's self-confidence and outlook on life. And even among peers, kids can be incredibly mean, not realizing how devastating their words can be, leaving behind an impact that can last a lifetime.

Traumatic events can flip our deserving switches off in a flash. Then similar patterns repeat themselves throughout our lives, only reinforcing the original undeserving belief, compounding the damage. No one escapes experiencing this, no matter how supportive or sheltered your upbringing may have been.

Parents, teachers, siblings, friends, bullies, TV, or anyone you ever came in contact with has the potential to plant an undeserving seed in your mind as a child. Indeed, most of your undeserving beliefs are due to whomever you were around the majority of your youth, *their beliefs transferred into your developing psyche.*

But seeds of undeserving are not just planted in us as children. They can develop at any age and in any area of life. Rachel was one of the very first doctors to work with me years ago. She already had quite a successful practice in California, but knew it could be even better. She had significant reservations about her fee structures. She also had concerns about what she was previously taught to say to her new patients. This caused her much inner doubt, which triggered self-sabotage. Why? Because she had an undeserving belief in this area professionally.

Within two months of working together and helping her shift her mind to a more patient-centered way of practice, she began making $10,000 more per month, and this continued on for years. The most interesting part is that she didn't increase her marketing, her hours, her services, or her staff. It was her mentality that had been shifted.

When she realized she could be comfortable and congruent with everything she said to her patients, her deserving belief for ever greater success provided the momentum she needed. And in turn, more patients referred to her, stayed with her, and invested in her.

If it seems too hard to look back through your childhood for where your undeserving beliefs began, you do not necessarily have to. It is very valuable to do so, but not necessary. What matters most is recognizing where you have these life hindering beliefs right now. Whether an undeserving belief developed in your youth and has been present for decades or if it was created just last year, the most important point is recognizing that it exists. Then you can apply The Deserving Process you will learn in the next chapter.

* * * * *

Growing up, even though I got A's in school and was most often the captain and a star athlete on my youth sports teams, I never felt I was good enough. I never thought I was "doing it right," especially not in my mother's eyes. She expected only the best from my older brother and me and seemed to have an impossibly hard to meet standard.

I would come home from school with a 95 test score and hear *"That's great. What happened to the other 5 though?"* Or, I would enthusiastically run through the front door carrying a shiny trophy exclaiming that we won the basketball tournament, having received the MVP award and scored 20 points and crushed the opponent, only to hear, *"Oh, I feel so bad for the other team."* I began to interpret this as, "My accomplishments are never good enough."

As far back as I can remember I heard my dad yelling at my mom, "Stop criticizing the boys!" It was said long before I even knew what the word "criticize" meant. But being critical was a parental technique my mother had mastered. She inherited this habit from her own mother who did the same to her.

To this day it's still hard for me to tell my mom what I'm happy or proud about in life because I'm expecting to get a response like, *"Well I don't know if that will last..."* or *"I'm concerned about that..."*

Even now, if she does compliment something about my life, there's a hesitancy in my response. I can almost feel my stomach muscles tightening as I am thinking to myself, "Is this compliment genuine or is she attempting to make up for not saying anything positive like it during my entire childhood?" It is an automatic mental reaction I cannot control, stemming from years of the experience.

When my mom reads this, she likely won't understand. Why? Because she doesn't know she's doing it and it's not intentional on her part. **For all of us, our behavioral and emotional responses are unconscious, automatic behaviors caused by years of conditioning.** Our young minds are so very malleable. Little do we know how these key events are creating a belief system that determines our destiny.

* * * * *

Needless to say, in light of what I have shared, I felt tremendous pressure growing up. This overarching theme of being not good enough and not doing it right hovered over me constantly. I was familiar with the concept of peace of mind, but I couldn't relate to it at all. I always felt as if everything I did was never enough, all of it in preparation for my future.

So all my studying was not done out of genuine pleasure, but only to get good grades so that I could get into a good college and get a well-paying job to attain financial security as an adult.

So what were all the years and countless hours of sports training and weightlifting all about? I knew I had to be *significant,* a captain, a leader, and that I had to win. That's just who I was supposed to be. Deep down, I resented having to prove myself and I was angry about it. No matter what I did, I still never felt good enough. My entire early life I felt pressure to create a future I couldn't even envision.

Looking back at my high school and college years it's no surprise that at the end of the week what I most craved was getting drunk with my friends. It was the only way I knew to escape the incessant pressure I put on myself.

Meanwhile, it seemed to me like being grown up was all about making sure you could afford your mortgage, take care of your kids, and take your family on vacation every year to escape the monotony of work and life's routine. I rarely saw husbands and wives having genuine fun or connecting with one another in a heartfelt way. My entire adolescence was a preparation for that future. Worse, I had to sacrifice enjoying my youth in order to ensure that I actually achieved it.

All these seminal experiences were essentially telling me *I don't deserve what I'm going for.* And it wasn't only my mother who was critical. Yes, my dad was not judgmental, but when it came to sports, all bets were off. On the basketball court he was the loudest to yell out his criticisms for any mistake I made. And he screamed at me so aggressively that I would be mortified, humiliated in front of my teammates and their parents.

True, he always supported my life decisions, but he had a blind spot when it came to sports, with unrelenting expectations about my athletic performance.

So what was supposed to be a childhood hobby and passion felt like training to be a Navy SEAL. In fact, there was little joy except for working out with teammates in preparation for a season or enjoying the celebrations after wins when we all hung out socially together.

Overall, as a youth, you might say that I was caught in the perfect storm, my life scrutinized and filled with pressure. My father overbearing of me in sports, my mother seemingly in virtually everything else I did. Not until my 30's did I start to realize that everything I was doing in almost every aspect of my life was based around always preparing for a future dictated by others' expectations. Therefore, I was rarely enjoying or living in the present.

For most people, the undeserving beliefs that dominate their lives are a direct result of early programming, whether related to relationships and money, health or career.

It could have been you hearing, "Who's going to pay for that?" over and over by your parents when you asked for the latest birthday toy or a trip to Disney World. Maybe it was the old standby, "Money doesn't grow on trees." Or it could have been as straightforward as "We can't afford that" or "That's not for us."

So your financial undeserving belief does not necessarily evolve from a single event. It usually comes from years of repetition, conditioning inside your childhood home. The dinner table talk from your parents, the house you lived in, the cars you drove, and the vacations you were taken on were all representations of your family's concept of money. Over time, the circumstances of your environment led you to believe that this is the lifestyle you're deserving of, *even when you grow up and are on your own.*

At five years old, I'm in the back of my parents' car, coming home from an afternoon trip. It's a long ride and my brother to my left is already asleep. I'm trying to fall asleep.

In front of me is my mother, her head tilted against the window, playing with her hair, which has always indicated a nervous habit. My father is driving. I notice tension and an argument starts to build between them, which wouldn't have happened if they knew I was awake.... but I looked like I was asleep.

This argument happened to be about money, which was a recurring theme. The tension builds as my father asks questions and vents his frustration, while my mother stays silent. Then, finally, one sentence is said by my father, left indelible in my mind. In exasperation and exhaustion, I hear my father say, "We don't have any money left." It was silence after that, or at least I don't remember anything more.

Back at home, there was nothing prepared for dinner, so my father asks us "Would you like me to order pizza?" I crawl up on his lap, while he's sitting on the couch, and say, "Dad, how do we order pizza if we don't have any money?" He dismisses it and says, "It'll be all right," and takes me off his lap.

From that moment, I knew I would never let money stress me out. I saw the most powerful figure in my life look broken, overwhelmed and stressed because of money, and I knew I never wanted to live like that.

Not feeling there was enough money showed up in my childhood. I was always finding ways to earn, whether through odd jobs, raking and mowing neighbors' lawns and shoveling driveways, seasonal tag sales on my front lawn, or even taking handouts from my grandparents. In short, finances were always on my mind. In fact, my mother saved a birthday card I sent to my grandmother because it was so funny and indicative of this mentality. It reads:

"Happy birthday Grandma Margie, I hope you have a nice day. I like sleeping at your house. I hope I could do it again soon. This year for my birthday instead of a present, I want $75 like you gave to Max (my younger cousin) and tell my other grandparents to do the same. I mean call my other grandparents and tell them. I hope you have a nice day. Love"

This was a birthday card *to* my grandmother!

As I grew into adulthood, I didn't care about having more wealth than those around me, or showing off what I earned. I just wanted to have enough so I would never have to worry. In short, my financial life was conditioned from my experience at a young age, and I kept to my promise—not wanting money to *ever* be a source of stress in my life. This has been a motivating factor that explains my diligence, self-discipline, and an overall sense of responsibility regarding the money I make and how I live my life financially.

* * * * *

How do you know what your undeserving beliefs are? The easiest way is to look objectively at every area of your life. Each is a reflection of what you believe you deserve. Emotionally, do you approach your day and your life with a sense of gratitude, joy, and wonder? Or do you get out of bed with a sense of pessimism or even fear of your day? Romantically are you in a relationship that inspires? Or are you unhappy and feel trapped? Or maybe you go from one relationship to another, repeating the same pattern again and again. Financially does it feel like you'll never make it work out? Or do you feel grateful for the amount of wealth present in your life right now?

If you know you don't want the rest of your life to continue as it is, then your next step is choosing which area you most want to change. Make it a priority and then FLIP YOUR SWITCH! You weren't born believing you were undeserving. Understand that these beliefs originated in childhood. And you can get past them. How? By turning on your deserving belief. And it is important to find out where it got turned off.

Chapter 4 Most Important Takeaways

- Your behavior and emotional responses are mostly unconscious. They are reactions to your beliefs that were influenced by your environment, upbringing and by traumatic events. As time passed, your responses were conditioned deeper, reinforced throughout your life.
- The people who influenced your undeserving beliefs most likely did not do so intentionally.
- Your childhood is not the *only area* undeserving beliefs can arise. At any point in life you can fall victim to undeserving beliefs, or, choose to create new deserving ones.
- In order to flip your switch, you should identify the originating causes of your undeserving beliefs. At a minimum, you must be able to be aware of where they are right now.
- You *can* have powerful deserving beliefs beginning in your childhood.

Chapter 4

Workbook For Deservingness

Use the Chapter 4 worksheet in the online resources to help you locate the earliest example of undeserving beliefs in your life. It may seem hard at first, but this worksheet will quickly clarify the things in childhood your unconscious never forgot.

When are you most aware of your undeserving beliefs? Can you notice any persistent repeated patterns that result in making you feel those negative feelings about what you deserve?

Chapter 5

Flip The Switch:
Taking Back Your Happiness

I began a personal practice of meditating during my college years at NYU. You could say it was my "old college try." I did it randomly whenever I had the time and if I was in the mood. No schedule. No specific approach.

I'd sit with my eyes closed and try not to think. Arguably, NOT thinking, for me, was the hardest thing to do. Later on in graduate school, the consistency of my meditation increased, but I still had no idea what I was doing. Eventually I did start researching the science behind meditation, specifically the efficacy of Transcendental Meditation, a specific form of silent mantra-based meditation.

After grad school, consumed with stress and anxiety about where I would set up my practice, meditation failed me miserably. I would attempt to quiet my mind, but the incessant negative and fearful thoughts only intensified. So, I stopped meditating altogether.

Upon beginning my practice, I felt even more stressed because I was a first-time business owner pulled in countless directions, doing everything on my own initially without staff. Thankfully, I realized it was time to start meditating again to gain more focus and clarity. But I did it for real this time —a committed and diligent discipline scheduled into my day.

The same month I heard Oprah endorsing Transcendental Meditation (TM) and there was a special offer for the weekend course to learn the technique. To me, the fee was substantial, $1,500, but it was discounted to $1,000. I grabbed it. The goal was to learn a life-changing 20-minute meditation routine.

After the course, I did the twice-daily routine just as instructed. All in all, there were no major shifts experienced in my first couple of weeks. If I hadn't paid to learn it, I would have quit. Forty minutes each day with all I already had on my plate was a lot to sacrifice not to see an immediate positive difference.

But about a month into it I started to notice real changes. I had more focus during my day, especially in the afternoon and evening. Most important were the inner changes—I wasn't as self-critical as I used to be, nor was I as hard on others. I wasn't taking setbacks as seriously, which was my lifelong modus operandi. All these changes were like getting a gorilla off my back. I now felt more calm and focused. And from this point forward I never missed the meditations (partially out of fear of losing what I'd gotten from them).

If I had quit earlier on, I never would have experienced these shifts. It was like benefiting from years of therapy by just meditating for 20 minutes twice each day. For the next three years, I enjoyed the benefits of TM, and to this day I am grateful for having chosen that initial meditation path. I also know if it weren't for that initial investment I wouldn't have stayed committed to it. And who knows how life would have progressed?

However, over time my personal results with TM plateaued. I began exploring other kinds of self-healing, learning the unique benefits and purpose of each. But regardless of what I tried, in the last decade, not a day has gone by that I haven't done at least 20 minutes of meditation. It is inconceivable to me to not start my morning with it, and I know it is a practice I will never let go of the rest of my life. The benefits of meditation have grown exponentially as I have evolved and it is my most important daily routine. But what does this all have to do with *your* deserving beliefs?

Undeserving beliefs have likely been present in your psyche for decades. Flipping your switch is simple, but not necessarily easy. It takes commitment and diligence. You're going to get the tools here to undo years of negative mental conditioning.

You'll experience psychological barriers disintegrating and procrastination fading away. You will attract into your life the right people and resources to nurture you. You will find yourself inspired to move forward with new ideas, unconstrained by fear. Even while doing some of the same things you always do, you will produce different results. Along the way, you'll be feeling more optimistic about yourself, your life, and your future.

To regain your deserving belief, you must first commit to a daily practice of The Deserving Process. This process you can do from the comfort of your own home at any time you like.

The three-step Deserving Process consists of:
1. **Sensing**

2. **Clearing**
3. **Emotionalizing**

* * * * *

Step 1: Sensing

Sensing is a simple first step allowing you to ease into a meditative state giving you the ability to better connect with your body before the more important next two steps.

In a seated position (never lying down) with all distractions removed (cell phone on airplane mode, no computer notifications within earshot) and eyes closed, start to sense your physical body. Sensing is *not* just feeling. Sensing is connecting and listening to the energy and internal state of your entire physical being. Mentally scan over your hands and arms, your legs, your chest, your entire core, sensing each area's internal presence.

When sensing is done intently, you will notice a subtle vibration, a pulsation in your body. It may feel like the blood coursing through your veins and arteries of your extremities. It may be the silent rhythm of the energy inside your body you are only aware of when you get truly quiet and intent on noticing it.

Sensing is not feeling the temperature of your skin or the contact of your body with your chair. That is too superficial. The purpose is to mentally scan your pure physicality. We live in a culture of high distraction. This step begins the process for two minutes, allowing you to detach from the noise of the world and reconnect to your physical body.

* * * * *

Step 2: Clearing

What I'm about to share with you will probably not make sense until you experience it. I have followed this method for years in order to dissolve resentments, mental barriers, and fears and can attest firsthand to the efficacy of this practice. Once you learn and do it, you will too.

You cannot create a new deserving belief on top of an undeserving one, just as you cannot build a beautiful home on top of a swamp. Sure, you can have the perfect architectural layout and designs for a gorgeous new home, but if the property is on top of a sinkhole, it will never take shape.

For almost a year, every morning my meditation practice was completely hijacked. Nothing moved forward in my life and a mild depression set in. I couldn't shake it. Compounding my distress was a bad business decision: I had made a substantial financial loan to a friend for his business startup. And as so many tend to discover, especially in business, not everyone is who they seem to be. Not all promises are kept, even signed ones. After being endlessly double-talked and sworn repayment for two years, I realized it was not going to ever happen. I'd been taken.

It was not the loss of all the money that hurt me as it was the feeling of disloyalty. I felt betrayed, taken advantage of and completely disrespected. Worse, it was done by someone I had considered a friend and mentor. The agony of not knowing how to proceed was compounded by my feeling powerless.

Lawyers I spoke with didn't want to get involved in what could wind up being a drawn-out case resulting in little to no monetary return. Anxiety and anger consumed me every time the issue popped into my head countless times each day. Every morning, I awakened to thoughts like these: *"How am I going to get the money back?" "How did I get myself into this?"* and of course *"What did I do to deserve this?"*

These thoughts would begin to bombard my mind during my morning meditation. And once the negative thoughts popped in my entire routine was thrown off. I was in this stressed state for an entire year, missing my deep and peaceful meditation. No longer did I have the focus, energy, and emotional calm I was used to. My business and personal life both suffered.

And then, fortuitously, I was introduced to a retired minister and a therapist named Pat Palmer who had developed a transformative technique designed to dissolve persistent stressful emotions, outlined in her book, *The Clearing Process*.

In the process, you go back into your past, re-experiencing the emotions from childhood—powerlessness, disrespect, and betrayal—or whatever else you might have experienced that caused pain, fear, or anxiety. The negative situation you're currently in is actually an invitation to finally heal the old repressed emotions you've been carrying for life.

When you use The Clearing Process, the focus is NOT on what to do about your current situation; in fact, taking action toward it can actually distract from the healing process. Nor is the purpose of Clearings to figure out WHY something happened to you. Would you agree that some people could have lost money in the same way as I did, yet could have reacted quite differently? Some might have wiped their hands clean and walked away without sinking into a depression, with ruined mornings and lack of focus throughout their day. Of course, I knew that was possible for me too. But I was trapped, stuck in recurring negative thought patterns consuming my day and sabotaging my mood.

That is why Clearing is so important. It's like a computer re-set to clear out emotions that no longer serve you and clog up your operating system, so to speak. You need to have a blank slate to move forward and create the new emotions, as a foundation for the life you most desire.

This loan situation was not the first time I experienced such pronounced negative feelings and hurt. **By the time you reach your mid-thirties, you've experienced most of the emotions life offers.** My sense of powerlessness, being taken advantage of and disrespected stemmed from early childhood events.

It was from there I went to work clearing each one. I realized that these were deeply ingrained emotions that had continually resurfaced throughout my life, ones that I had never addressed.

I now saw that I didn't have to be angry or feel betrayed anymore. Through using Clearings, 90 percent of the emotional strain cleared away. I was able to resume my daily meditation without interference and had a new level of calmness, gratitude, and peace.

I also saw both sides of situations more clearly. I came to understand why parental choices were made when I was a child and I could now feel forgiveness. I no longer felt the actions of others were a personal assault against me. I saw what had happened as a blessing, an experience for which I could choose to be grateful. And believe it or not, when I found out the company I gave the loans to was finally making money (though I still was not being paid back) I actually felt happy their business was now viable.

This healing is what I want for you to experience in any area of your life where you feel deep emotional pain. We all have ingrained negative emotions that are brewing inside us, preventing us from true peace of mind and moving forward in life courageously. **There's no escaping this because, again, no one gets out of childhood unscathed.** The only issue is how intensely these fears, stresses and anxieties are interfering with your ability to produce the life you want now.

Of course, stress is a fundamental part of life, though it's relative depending upon the event. Childhood trauma from sexual or physical abuse will obviously spark different emotional blocks in adulthood than those of a child who received an inadvertent unloving comment from a parent. Yes, both may result in similar undeserving emotional beliefs, though the emotional scars and impact in their lives are quite different.

A mother telling a daughter she doesn't need another sugary snack before dinner could easily instill a belief she's overweight and should not eat so much. It could go deeper and instill an undeserving belief about her body, leading to self-esteem issues when it comes to dating and overall self-worth. How that will show up is unique to each individual, whether it is a mild self-consciousness, an eating disorder, or a life profoundly affected by abusive relationships.

Even if you cannot recall traumatic instances in your childhood it doesn't mean you are not holding deep negative emotions and undeserving beliefs within, ones that were formed subtly over the years and then compounded throughout your life.

Take the example of the mom who never thought you were beautiful. You grow up believing that you don't deserve anyone who thinks you're beautiful. Or, you felt your dad didn't earn the income or achieve the lifestyle he could be proud of, so now you don't think you deserve an income or lifestyle you can be proud of either.

Through Clearing, we can finally let go of the resentment and anger toward others and replace it with forgiveness, love, gratitude and appreciation for our current life. **No longer will we be held captive by our past negativity, which inhibits us from creating the future we most want.** In each area you apply The Deserving Process you'll go from feeling stuck to free, from lack to abundance.

Clearing isn't about others. It's not about what happened to you. It's about freeing yourself from being trapped by your negative emotions so they stop continually resurfacing. In short, it's time to move past the negative emotions that create your strained relationships and your staying stuck in life.

I'm not telling you, however, that Clearings will permanently rid you of ever having a negative emotion again. That's not real life. But it will finally allow you to deal with your deepest and most intensely negative emotions that act as roadblocks to your happiness.

No longer will you find yourself entangled in unsupportive relationships or situations that don't affirm your worth. **Clearing will free you from unconsciously creating these unwanted circumstances.** The Deserving Process gives you the ability to create anew. You'll see that the way your life turns out isn't random. Your life isn't "happening" *to you*, as much as it may feel like that now.

Taking the 5-10 minutes to clear your negative emotions as part of the Deserving Process will dramatically free up much of your day and provide greater clarity of mind. It will also give you more space for creative thoughts and new life plans, since the weight of your negative emotions have already been dealt with. It is a vital step that must be performed before creating the future you desire.

If you don't deal with your negative emotions, they will deal with you. Doing this work will free you from self-sabotage, denial, feeling stuck or burnt out. No longer will you believe that you're a victim, that you don't have any control over people or circumstances around you.

* * * * *

So how exactly do you do Clearings? I will show you now. This will probably sound counter-intuitive. It may even bother you so much that you won't want to even try it. But I ask you to trust me. This works, even though it is not comfortable.

Identify one primary place where you experience emotional pain, resentment, or fear. Any of these can prevent you from moving forward and creating the future you want. Once you have done Sensing in Step 1, to properly do Step 2, Clearing, create a crystal-clear vision, a movie in your mind of exactly what causes you this emotional stress.

If it involves your negative emotions surrounding money, clearly picture your paycheck, your bank account balance, your debt collection bills or even your perceived competition outperforming you.

For me, the images that filled my mind included the face of my friend who did not return the loan and the sound of voicemail recordings of his other business partner screaming that I stop seeking the money.

With your eyes closed, the more intensely you can channel these emotions the better. The goal is for you to reignite these unwanted, negative emotions and allow them to surface in your body to fully experience them. This will not feel comfortable.

When it comes to the subject of love, the pain related to undeserving beliefs can be unfathomable. Re-experience the pain and hurt you felt from the breakups of your past, the anguish you felt when you were stuck or trapped in the wrong relationship, or the loneliness of not having a partner in life.

When you close your eyes and begin your visualization, hurtful emotions will resurface quickly. Most of the time, of course, we bury these painful feelings and, instead, distract ourselves with food, alcohol, drugs, TV, socializing, sex, the gym, or what you do to escape the areas of your life that need changing. It is the survival mechanism our minds are wired for in order to protect us from past pain. But what protects you in the short-term can ultimately destroy you in the long-term. And life is a long-term game.

While doing a Clearing, if you resist the emotion that appears, it will never leave your life and instead continue to dominate you. It will own you and create a life that continually re-creates those negative emotions, bombarding you with them throughout the day, often at the worst possible times. **It will also create events and circumstances that reproduce the emotion for you to experience, since you have not cleared it.**

When you try to bury these emotions deep down or constantly avoid them, you are in denial. But the more you can choose to experience the emotions you don't want, the less grip they will have on you. Once you've fully experienced the emotions, they have served their purpose and can move on.

It is critical that you not delude yourself into thinking that the current person or situation causing negative feelings is the source of your pain; *they are only the catalyst.* You only focus on them in the Clearing visualization to help you get in touch with those feelings that were first created—likely at a young age. You cannot get into blaming or feeling like a victim; *that will keep you stuck.*

When you do Clearings related to your childhood experiences, it is important to recognize that undeserving beliefs were instilled in you by your parents, siblings, or whoever was involved. Blame may be appropriate. And yes, as just a child, you were a victim. Now, however, you need to feel that pain, fear, anger or sadness fully.

Throughout Clearings your mind will fight you. You will notice how the visualization process is often interrupted by daydreaming, another mind defense that allows you to evade the feeling. That's normal. When you notice your mind wandering, just return to bringing the negative visualization back, and the emotion will return.

Think of it as a workout. A challenging physical workout provides more benefit and the same applies here. If you are going to do the Clearing, go all out. This is your life and future you are fighting for. Clearly it is true that some memories may be too painful to go back and feel all at once. Approach the work gradually in cases of severe trauma.

When you can hold that same original negative scene in your mind and note a large percentage of the negative emotion has disappeared, you are done with the Clearing for that session. Now you can move on to Step 3 of The Deserving Process.

This doesn't mean the negative feeling will be gone forever. But it does mean that the Clearing session is complete. In a short amount of time after doing The Deserving Process, you will notice your mind and attitude are no longer bombarded randomly throughout the day with negative emotions, *even if the stressful issue is still present in your life.*

You will have a new perspective on stressors and, when needed, forgiveness will arise. You will not unconsciously react to the person or situation with resentment or worry. Instead, you will come up with new ways on how to approach a difficult situation rather than being on autopilot, reverting to old forms of acting out negative emotions.

As you engage in the Clearings, keep each session focused on one of your undeserving beliefs at a time. In other words, don't combine money with relationships, or career with physical health. Stick with one major life sector at a time to build up the most traction.

In The Deserving Process, you will intuitively know when it's time to move on to the next area to clear because the current issue in your life will have shifted dramatically or you will no longer be feeling negative emotions that had enveloped you for so long. Stick with one area daily until you reach this resolution point, then move on to the next. As you see your life change, you will be excited and determined to continue on to overcome your next underserving belief.

* * * * *

Step 3: Emotionalizing

As potent and powerful as meditation can be, most techniques fall short on their own to produce the results you want in life. The Law of Attraction states that if you can see what you want with clarity, and focus on it enough, you will have the ability to manifest it in your life. Unfortunately, that's not true. It's only one piece of a larger puzzle. And just like any equation, if you're missing one piece, *it won't equal the end result you're after.*

How many years can you go on visualizing your bank account growing or the big promotion happening? You envision complete financial freedom, yet you remain stuck in the same situation with no breakthrough happening. I wish it could be as easy as just closing your eyes and seeing what you want, *but it's not.*

There is a missing factor beyond meditation that can ignite your brain to create the shift you need: **It's the ability to flip your subconscious switch from undeserving to deserving.** It's what causes everything in your life to change. Knowing deep within that you deserve what you desire automatically allows you to move forward to get it.

What's the one missing element that can make all the difference? Emotion —the force that drives all our thoughts, decisions, and actions. Emotion is the source of energy that moves all people. **Emotion is the secret ingredient that moves a vision to reality.** Without emotion, you can robotically stare at your vision board or read your list of goals over and over again, and little will ever change. **Without emotion, we don't take action.**

During visualization, accessing strong emotion will give you the energy to act on what you need to do. It will fuel ideas with inspiration, allowing you to take the best action possible, even if you did not know what to do beforehand.

When you activate your emotional core, you'll start seeing results. The people around you will notice something different about you too. Suddenly, you're more vital and alive. Emotion shows up in your total being—in your body posture, your tone of voice, your walk, smile, and facial expressions. All these elements shift without you even realizing it. When you begin bringing emotion into your visualizations, you'll start to feel better as you go through your day, even before anything else you do changes. Just *that* is a tremendous gift to your life.

*****

Gratitude is the most powerful emotion for creating the life you want. Being thankful signifies to your powerfully creative subconscious mind that you already have what you are grateful for. Even if your vision is not yet realized, if you are grateful for what you DO have, that feeling will lead toward more. In turn, your gratitude will drive you to act in alignment with actually having what it is you desire, even if you don't yet have it. The key is feeling as if you have it, in advance.

So, try this easy trick. Cultivate gratitude in advance for what you want. Your subconscious then causes you to act in the precise ways to attract and create it in your life. This is subtle yet profound. It applies to relationships, health, wealth, or any area of life. Focused and daily gratitude and appreciation cause and enable you to act in the way needed to produce what you are being grateful for.

Even though gratitude is the most important emotion of visualization, it is not the only one to use in Step 3 of The Deserving Process. You can focus also on choosing the emotions your newly visualized life will provide you.

The romantic relationship likely ignites the feelings of being loved and in love. Financial abundance or your dream job may lead to feelings of accomplishment, a sense of freedom, and excitement. Getting to your ideal weight may allow you to finally be at peace with your body and have more confidence.

In each case, when you concentrate intently on your new vision, you can predict what emotion you are going to feel. These emotions, including gratitude, are what you must use in your Step 3: *Emotionalization.*

This isn't as easy as it sounds. You have never been taught to create your emotions on command. **Throughout your entire life you're conditioned to *feel* an emotion only after something happens that causes you to react.** But emotions don't just happen *to* us. Instead, they are actually a result of what we *think* is happening to us.

For example, we feel happy after we receive a gift, so long as we believe it was a genuine gesture. We feel loved after someone tells us something loving, so long as we believe it is sincere. We feel excited when we think about a party we're looking forward to attending. We feel confident when we get what we believe is a true compliment.

In fact, we have more control over our emotional state than we think we do. **Being powerful and in control of your destiny is the ability to channel the feelings you want before the events you most want appear.** This is the secret element that turns your visualization into *emotionalization* for creating new results. It's what spiritual texts have advocated for centuries.

A commitment to Emotionalization is the final step to flip your switch from undeserving to deserving using The Deserving Process. You will start to align your emotions with your environment in order to bring into your life what you focus on. As you move through your daily routine, no longer will you feel as if you have a thousand pounds on your back without any hope for the future.

Instead, you will notice new freedom. Your life is now aligned to your newfound deserving belief rather than being held captive to old habits. This change can show up as newfound optimism and increased physical energy, both of which lead you toward unexpected opportunities. You will know you are on your way to having what you want by your upbeat mentality, the flood of new ideas, and the new actions you take. You will also begin to attract the right people. You will notice that life is conspiring to put the right opportunities directly in your path.

Remember, you are not limited to what your life looks and feels like right now. It might feel as if you can never escape it, but that is not the case. True, if you do nothing new, you can be sure nothing will change. Begin The Deserving Process today. Make it a daily habit and watch what starts happening.

Step 3 of The Deserving Process is practicing emotionalization for approximately ten minutes once your Step 2 Clearing comes to a natural conclusion. You will feel a subtle blank slate of emotion as negativity reduces and passes. This is the ideal time to generate gratitude and appreciation, which will allow you to create a new mental picture, or movie, of how you want your life to look and feel like.

The longer you can sustain the positive emotion and the vision the better. You will inevitably find yourself daydreaming at times. That is to be expected. When this happens, simply return to the positive emotion of your vision. You'll discover that when you access deep emotions, the exercise leaves you feeling renewed. It is a gift to yourself.

So just as physical exercise releases endorphins making you feel great after the pain and burn of the muscle workout, emotionalization also generates optimism, enthusiasm, and excitement. As you continue the daily practice, the positive emotions will be present for longer times between sessions.

* * * * *

Throughout your life, one of the most potent pathways to emotional healing is forgiveness. Brain mapping or fMRI (Functional Magnetic Resonance Imaging) studies have proven how the brain changes after cultivating true forgiveness.

And if you don't forgive? Well, it's been said not forgiving someone is like drinking poison and waiting for the other person to die. Holding onto resentment is only harmful to you, not the person you resent.

The ultimate sign of an undeserving mindset is *not forgiving*. Wherever you are not willing to forgive, you are acknowledging you don't deserve peace in that area of your life. And you know my stance on the importance of peace of mind.

There are many ways to cultivate forgiveness. The Deserving Process will assist you tremendously here.

One Sunday years ago, I stumbled upon a center in Manhattan dedicated to spiritual growth, so I stopped in to listen to a lecture. Jack was a teacher who worked there and led the discussion. It happened to be on forgiveness.

I left that Sunday afternoon with an incredibly valuable and unexpected insight. Someone important in your life has likely hurt you so badly you haven't forgiven them. The hurt and unwillingness to forgive sits deep within you. It's burdensome. It affects your mood. In fact, you have no idea how much it's sabotaging your peace of mind and entire life, let alone your relationship (or lack of) with that once-special person.

Whether you call it karma or cause and effect, Jack made it clear that life works itself out and we all have what is coming to us. For example, whoever hurt you is naturally dealing with the effects of their actions, *even if you can't see it or know it is happening*. If you've been scorned, it is easy to think that person has gotten off the hook and is dancing their way through life right now. I guarantee you they are not. For one, they've lost having you in their life. That alone is often a major sacrifice.

Jack then eloquently described that we are not responsible for delivering the punishment or "effect" these people deserve. Take yourself off the hook for being the force that has to right their wrongs, and understand it happens naturally. Then it is far easier to forgive.

Forgiveness does not erase what they did. It does not make it okay. Rather, it makes it okay for you to not keep suffering because of it. **It is taking your**

power back and not allowing the pain to dictate your future happiness like it has before. Your reward is you getting your life back.

It can be incredibly valuable to look at people in your life whom you're unwilling to forgive. Instead, apply this mentality: *Thank you for giving me this experience.* That sounds counter-intuitive. **But anything, no matter how traumatic, can be a learning experience if you choose it to be one.** This does not discredit the hurt or suffering it may have caused you. It does allow you, however, to extract positivity from it and help you address your undeserving beliefs.

For example, it has been challenging to write about the experiences of my upbringing and fears about what my family or even others might think. However, through doing these processes around forgiveness, I realized my mother has been one of my greatest teachers throughout life, despite her habit of undermining my efforts.

In the past, my mother would take every opportunity to question my personal choices. I would become very reactive and defensive towards her while masking my hurt. Through my work with The Deserving Process, even at times when I was tempted to express an intense emotional response towards my mother, I learned to go from blaming her shortcomings and instead asking myself about my own character defects.

This led to me to understand myself in a much deeper way. I gradually felt free of resentment and blame, ultimately rectifying the relationship between my mother and me—a relationship I cherish today. I can see the significant role she played in my development and I am forever grateful.

Does she still rile me up at times? Of course. However, the tension between us has been reduced by 95 percent. Even when it does happen, I look within to find a lesson. "Where am I avoiding something I should be looking at in my life?" I wind up being thankful for the lesson I find, able to now accept my mother's love (which she expresses in her unique way). Thanks Mom.

* * * * *

The evidence for the beneficial and long-lasting effects of meditation has been proven in a plethora of scientific studies.[1] And the research by Chavez et al. (2015) indicates it is possible to instill the belief of deservingness too, seen through actual brain structure changes. This is startling: You can literally change the physical aspects of your brain by flipping your switch and putting in the work, although it does take more extended training until these physical effects are noticeable.

The conclusion from psychological research: your unconscious belief in deservingness moderates your behavior without you even knowing it. Of course, even if you do everything you can to achieve success your negative unconscious beliefs will inevitably hamper your growth. But, if you can train your mind toward positive emotion, just as you build your muscles in the gym, the result will be a transformed state of mind.

Brain experiments using neuroimaging have demonstrated that with longer training, scientists observed real structural differences in the neuroanatomy of the brain.[2] Meaning you actually can develop higher self-esteem and train your unconscious belief in deservingness—*but only when you work diligently for it.*

Commit to The Deserving Process daily and you can change your brain to work for you, rather than against you, to create the life you desire.

The 3 Step Deserving Process
Summary and Best Practices:

Don't allow anything to interrupt your 20 minute process. Put your phone on airplane mode so you receive absolutely no notifications. If you are within notification sound of a computer, move or turn the volume off. Do not begin the process immediately after eating and *never* do it lying down (because it is too easy to fall asleep). Keep a paper and pen beside you for ideas that come to you that should be written down. If you attempt to remember these ideas for later, it will interfere with the rest of your process.

When you feel great about the emotion you have generated in your Step 3 Emotionalization, open your eyes and look at the clock. If it is not yet 20 minutes, keep going until you look again and it is. If you are just past 20 minutes, you can finish and proceed with your day.

* * * * *

1. Initial Sensing (2 minutes)

In a comfortable, SEATED position with hands on your lap begin to *SENSE* your body. Sensing is *NOT* feeling. You are not feeling the temperature of the room nor the feeling of your skin on your clothing or chair. Sensing is being aware of your body's internal sensation. You may feel a pulsing of the part of your body you are focusing on, like a heartbeat present. Give attention everywhere by mentally scanning your extremities and your core.

* * * * *

2. Clearing (5 to 10 minutes)

After connecting to your body through sensing, evoke your strongest visual and or auditory memory of the circumstance contributing to your strongest undeserving belief. The recollection of the person or circumstance should be strong enough to elicit the hurtful, negative emotion in your body easily and quickly. Add to this by intensifying the emotion, for instance, squeezing your stomach muscles as you focus on creating the negative feeling, or even vocalizing out loud what is happening in the scene.

As a beginner you'll find that your mind is easily distracted and often drifts away during this exercise. Don't let that discourage you. Every time you realize you are no longer feeling the negative emotion or visualizing the memory, come back to it and re-generate the negative feeling.

Sustain the vision and feeling for as long as possible. It's not easy to do and the more you do this process, the longer you will be able to hold the vision and emotion during a session. Once you notice the emotional tension has decreased significantly, you can move to Step 3. That negative emotion does not have to be gone entirely to move onto Step 3, just diminished.

* * * * *

3. Emotionalizing (10 minutes)

After Clearing, you will find it far easier to visualize and feel the emotions of what you want to experience in life. You have just wiped clean your emotional state, which makes it far easier to generate new positive emotions. Start picturing what you most want (in the same area of life you just cleared) and generate the emotion this vision gives you. Is it gratitude, joy, excitement, peace? Whatever single emotion your vision most generates, focus on it while holding the vision.

To intensify your emotion, breathe deeply into your chest and focus on gratitude even more intently. Once you sense an internal shift of newfound confidence in your vision and it has been 20 minutes, gently come out of the process. Continue on with your day and if you wrote down any notes during the process, make sure to take them seriously and act on them.

There's an astute saying: "If you don't have 20 minutes a day to meditate, *then you should be meditating for 40.*" It's not much to ask. You can surely find 20 minutes somewhere in your busy day. Even if you have three children who wake up earlier than you do, you can find time, like thousands of parents do, to nurture yourself with this practice somewhere in your daily schedule. **Your children too will benefit from your new mindset and perspective.**

Keeping the same time each day provides a predictable routine and habit that makes it easier to strengthen your commitment. So if possible, do The Deserving Process first thing in the morning. It is a phenomenal way to begin each day.

To support your effort, consider getting an accountability partner—a spouse, friend, or family member—who can do this process with you and share your journey. Their support and participation are an invaluable asset. Invite someone to read this book at the same time you do and begin the process together. It makes a tremendous difference not to be alone through it. Your commitment to not letting your partner down will strengthen your commitment to yourself. It's a win-win. Help someone you care about to flip their switch and it will expedite you flipping your own.

* * * * *

Chapter 5 Most Important Takeaways

- Your undeserving beliefs will not transform on their own. If you keep going through life the exact same way, *why would anythi*ng change?
- So often, the trigger that brings you current emotional strain is not the real issue or culprit at all. It's merely a re-creation of the emotional trauma that was never dealt with during your early childhood.
- The Deserving Process can be applied to your current present day stresses and emotional hurts just as much as the ones you find from your childhood.
- Clearings are not designed to blame others or for you to see yourself as an adult victim. However, you acknowledge that as a child you couldn't speak up for yourself, so you were a victim. And now, once again, you've fully experienced that emotion as an adult likely in a different circumstance, cleared it, and can move on.
- Remember, visualization without emotion does not create the internal change necessary to flip your switch and transform your life. Step 3: Emotionalization is key for your true deservingness to take hold.
- The Deserving Process is a phenomenal way to cultivate forgiveness, the greatest gift you can give yourself for healing and peace of mind.
- Remember you are not doing this only for yourself, but for everyone who is affected by you. Your deservingness and peace of mind helps bring out the same in people you touch.
- Knowing and understanding the significance of the deserving belief is only the first step. Committing to The Deserving Process daily is how you create it.

Chapter 5

Workbook for Deservingness

Choose a regular time and place every day that you can commit to doing your 20-minute deserving process. First thing in the morning is best.
- My best location for least distraction is:
- My best time for least interruption and most focus is:
- How will my family, friends and work benefit from my progress?

Chapter 6

Six Steps To Protect Your Self Worth

One Tuesday evening, after a full day of writing, work and client correspondence I was at home in the kitchen, chopping up vegetables for a dinner salad. While dicing the cucumbers I realized I had an unscheduled hour after dinner before my weekly mentor call. I thought to myself how should I spend this hour?

All day I had been stuck inside and realized I hadn't shot baskets in a while. Playing basketball in an empty gym had always been a joyful meditation for me, one of my favorite hobbies. At the same time, my mind went to "It's only Tuesday, stay focused and enjoy basketball at the endof the week. Don't distract yourself from your progress today."

My mind (or a conditioned guilty conscience) thinks I only earn a break once everything in my work life is complete. That's been my default mentality throughout my life, a strict rule that made no real sense. So yes, I've always played hard, but after getting all my work done.

Yet, on this night, in a spark of insight, I heard a voice say, "If you will not give yourself this enjoyment right now, why would life give it to you sometime in the future?" I thought, you have to be *willing to give this to yourself first*. That wise voice whispering inside me stopped me cold.

I tried to make sense of it. It seemed too simple. But the more I grappled with it, the more I understood. *Why would life give me what I want if I can't or won't give it to myself?*

I realized if I kept denying myself what I wanted I would keep building the muscle of self-deprivation. And by doing so, this creates *less* reason for life to give me what I'm seeking.

The thought seemed so simple, yet profound. It is never easy to change old patterns. But that night, armed with an inspired outlook, I chose to play basketball! And I refused to allow guilt to stop me.

Afterward, I noticed a missed call from a prospective client and called him back. We spoke very briefly about working together, and he signed up for my highest level of coaching. It was one of the easiest and shortest prospect calls I had ever had. I do not believe that was accidental. In my perspective, I saw this occurrence as life rewarding me for choosing myself over self-sacrifice. And it worked! I felt better—so I *did* better.

There is no end to all the things we have yet to do. There is no final goal. Any accomplishment is usually followed by another door opening another challenge. It's inevitable. So you think you may have achieved your final goal--like getting engaged or married, or getting a coveted new job or losing 25 pounds—but there is always going to be another challenge ahead. There is no final end point where you can just coast through the rest of your life, with no care or worry.

It is the process of taking life one moment at a time that really counts. It is that ability to be in the present moment that determines how happy you're going to feel. So often, we self-sabotage by only feeling we'll be happy when we get to the finish line. Instead, you have to enjoy the journey, every step of the way, *not just the outcome.*

I can tell you that reaching your end goal always starts another journey of "not there yet," driving you toward the next goal. So after the short-term feeling of accomplishment wears off, usually two days later, at most, before you is another objective, another mission to tackle. You can read countless testimonials of people who have accomplished their ultimate dream. And not long after, their thoughts quickly change to "Is this it?" and "What's next?"

When I thought about holding myself back from shooting baskets for 45 minutes in between dinner and my call, I fell back into my habitual mindset about work. That wasn't inspiring. It felt like being 16 years old again, forced to do my homework instead of getting onto the field and playing sports.

But I had finally learned that enjoyment of life is not to be delayed. You can enjoy your work and your non-work time without neglecting your life responsibilities or relationships. **Had I not chosen to give myself that basketball break I would have continued building the muscle of self-deprivation and denial.**

And no matter how greatly my business increased I would never find the time to enjoy myself guilt-free. Why? Because I'd still be stuck in the mindset of "it's not enough" and "I don't deserve it." Remember: How you are feeling in this moment will be the same when your circumstances change, even when you get whatever it is you want.

You take yourself wherever you go. So changing how you feel you must first focus inward with The Deserving Process. *Hoping* your circumstances change will not create change.

If you're always waiting for life to give you the emotions of love, joy, gratitude, or excitement... you might as well start buying lotto tickets if your goal is to be wealthy.

Why would life give you anything you don't believe you deserve, especially when you are demonstrating you do not deserve it? Life won't. *The act of giving yourself the emotion you want FIRST is a sign that you believe you deserve to have the emotion.* Then life creates the circumstances for you to have it naturally.

This is the power of The Deserving Process. You create the emotions you want first internally, while Clearing out the negative ones sabotaging you, and then life supports you by giving you the circumstances to reinforce the positive emotions.

For readers who already understand this concept, I believe metaphysical occurrences are happening to us at all times correlated to our deepest beliefs. When you flip your switch, new opportunities will present themselves, ones that you haven't seen before, giving you more opportunities to act on. However, it is also because of your newfound deserving belief that you are now able to *see* these new circumstances, opportunities, and people coming into your life. Flipping your switch is essential.

The rest of this chapter is devoted to extra practices you can do alongside The Deserving Process for strengthening your newly created beliefs. IMPORTANT: These six steps *do not* take the place of The Deserving Process. On their own, they will unlikely completely flip your switch. Rather, once you flip your switch using the process, each of these steps should be used to strengthen your newfound belief. You can also start applying any or all of them right away while you are doing the daily Deserving Process.

* * * * *

Six Steps to Strengthen Your Deserving Belief
*To Be Done After or Alongside The Deserving Process

1. Connecting with Deservers

One of the most powerful ways to strengthen your deserving belief is by surrounding yourself with others who believe they deserve it too! This could be someone who has a thriving business, or a great marriage. Armed with deservingness, this person has attained a lifestyle and peace of mind or happiness you desire and do not yet have.

How do you find these people? How do you know who is self-deserving and who is not? Just look at their life. If someone has what you want and it's not temporary or a social media façade, it indicates they believe they deserve to have it. Otherwise, *they wouldn't* have it.

So you don't have to ask anyone or investigate. Just diligently observe them. And don't forget, people's lives are not always what they seem to be—whether it's a happy and loving-looking relationship in public, the appearance of wealth based on material possessions, or happiness and fulfillment based on Instagram and Facebook quotes. Be warned: *Behind every sunset selfie is often suffering.* Many people share with the world what they want others to see and believe.

So how do you surround yourself with people who are self-deserving? As adults who have busy lives and set routines it is not so easy to find a group of peers who will inspire you. I have mentors I speak with every single week. Each one of them is in my life because I'm inspired by the way they are living their lives. And they care enough to guide me—to challenge and inspire me to reach higher. So the time on the phone allows me to be stimulated by their energy and insight.

The people in your life who have their deserving flip switched on likely do not know they do. It's unconscious and innate. They don't even know what the term 'deserving belief' means. They're just fortunate that they have it. Just by talking to them you'll be stimulated by their energy. You'll be influenced by their personality, the ideas and topics they discuss, how they speak about their spouse and family, and by their decision-making process (whether they're choosing their financial portfolio or making a lifestyle choice).

Just by being around those who have what you want, you will feel positively influenced. Years ago, I spent a day with a colleague 30 years older who had had a very successful practice and owned several others. He truly enjoyed his life and was now directing his energy toward building online companies. He had a professional video studio in his basement and offered me the opportunity to use it to create videos for my program. I gladly accepted and showed up one morning after a three-hour train ride to his home.

After an entire day of shooting we finished with a meal together, and I learned a great deal about him. In everything he said he demonstrated such a positive attitude about his new projects, and about his wonderful marriage and children. In fact, as he dropped me off at the train to head back to NYC he told me that after 30 years of marriage he was more in love with his wife than ever. That night, he was about to meet her for happy hour. "And there's no other person in the world with whom I'd rather get a drink!" he exclaimed.

That really impressed me and re-emphasized the importance of choosing a life partner. I wanted my wife to be the first person I would choose to meet for happy hour 30 years into marriage!

A year later I found myself wanting more life and business guidance, so I emailed this same doctor and acknowledged how much I respected what he had accomplished in his life. I told him I would love to be in closer communication with him and was hoping for a once-a-month phone call. He accepted my request, and it turned into a weekly call where he shared what was going on in his life. Just from listening to him speak I gained a tremendous amount of insight about his values and business decision-making processes. This contact was invaluable.

Who in your life could *you* reach out to for a valuable connection? A regular dialogue with that person would be ideal. True, people's lives are busy, so they can't always schedule repeat calendar appointments. So when you reach out to others to increase your deservingness *make sure you're offering something of benefit and value to them.* Don't be a taker. That causes a drain, and you will not foster a relationship where others want to be around you.

You will be surprised how many people would be willing to give you their time and energy just because you asked, motivated by your genuine admiration for them. And, of course, there are some who offer this in a more formal coaching relationship, which can work effectively as well.

This is one of the most important reasons for attending live seminars. It's so easy to feel isolated in your own world, focused only on your own life and career with little connection to others. For those I coach and mentor, it's therapeutic and energizing for them to meet and interact with one another, often meeting even more successful people who are confident about their own sense of deservedness. Everyone participates in fun exercises designed to flip the switch. All this mixing together at live seminars rubs off on everyone, inspiring them to strengthen their own deserving belief for life success. For the more successful clients, influencing others actually strengthens their own deservedness.

Typically, after one of my live seminars, self sabotaging habits begin to dissipate. No longer do you indulge in excessive drinking, poor diet, or lack of exercise. Your previously negative life outlook and lack of focus transform into a more positive, optimistic state of being. Now you're laser-focused on bringing deservingness to the areas most important to you.

Consider using this approach as one part of strengthening your own deserving.

* * * * *

2. Your Daily Routine

Your lifestyle (financial, relationships, mindset, health) becomes harder to change the longer it remains entrenched in the same pattern. At a certain age, the conditions of your life start to atrophy, becoming fixed—no longer responsive to much change. Your physical health, income, general attitude, and the quality of your relationships seem to have plateaued.

So whether it's a marriage you have no intention of changing, or an income that only rises predictably alongside inflation, or a home you don't plan on moving from until you have to, or how you feel overall emotionally —you become accustomed to the same look and feel of your life. So every day for years on end, nothing changes.

For a majority of people this begins to happen as early as our late 20s, especially if children are in the picture and your focus becomes raising them. **The more years that go by with the same lifestyle, the harder it is to change.**

Your mentality becomes, *"This is how it is, this is how it will probably always be."* But change is always possible if you believe you deserve it. This is a crucial reason to get out of your mental and physical rut. You've got to shake up your environment and routine, even if just for a few days, to snap out of the syndrome of "this is how it always is and will be."

It's one main reason I travel so much and am always learning, even if I feel like I don't need to invest the time, energy, and money into the trip. I often project ahead of time, and think "I already know this," so there's no reason to go. But inside, I knew that was my own self-sabotage at work, challenging my need for growth.

So I always purposely plan ahead now, scheduling events I'll attend during the next quarter or two of the year. Too often in the past, I'd find out about a seminar or retreat at the last minute so it was too late to attend, either because it was sold out or I had other plans that conflicted with the date.

I know that if I don't continually put myself into a learning and growth environment my life becomes stagnant and fixed. This doesn't mean there's anything wrong with my life now. The point is that there is always room for growth and the ability to evolve as a person.

Likewise, most attendees during my live seminars register for the next seminar months in advance, even before the seminar is over. Why? For the same reason: to ensure they are always growing to experience the best life has to offer. They don't allow excuses, unforeseen circumstances or procrastination to get in their way.

* * * * *

3. Hearing You Deserve It

The next way to strengthen your deserving is hearing you deserve it aloud. By using the deserving question you'll learn later in this chapter, you are programming your mind into believing it. So you have a much better chance of getting it. Talking it makes it tangible. Likewise, when other people say you deserve what you are after, it can have tremendous power on your deserving belief.

When I was in college and discovered I wanted to become a chiropractor, I had little experience in the field. I interned over the summer with a practice that I felt was the most successful, shadowing the main doctor and his team, learning everything I could.

At the end of my second summer before leaving for grad school, we were all sitting in a circle at our Monday team meeting. The owner of the practice began praising me in front of everyone and announced that when I graduated, I already had a job waiting for me at his office. I was more than four years away from graduation, but I already had a position lined up!

I was so proud of myself. Later, in private in his office, he admitted he planned to transition into professional coaching and leave his practice altogether. At that point, he said he'd like me to take it over entirely. I vividly remember driving home that summer day on cloud nine.

The belief this mentor had in me fueled my entire graduate school experience. I was brimming with confidence, believing that I deserved to be incredibly successful in practice. I would not have had that level of optimism and drive if he hadn't said what he did about my future potential and available position.

No matter how tough or monotonous grad school became, his words kept me going. He helped me see a bright light at the end of the tunnel no matter what the challenge.

Being around those who believe in you can have a profound impact on your performance and self-confidence. Their viewpoint rubs off on you.

If you're hesitant or feel weird about asking a friend or colleague to be your mentor, consider this—almost anyone who has what they want in life isn't in a mindset of scarcity or self-doubt. Nor are they fearful of competition. They don't see your talent or ambition as taking anything away from them (whether it's earning a million dollars or having peace of mind). Most who believe they're deserving understand that it is their natural right. So, of course, they will tell you that you deserve it too.

Does that mean that hard work and patience won't be necessary? Not at all! But just hearing them tell you they believe you deserve success will strengthen your own believing, causing you to be more disciplined, diligent, and focused on your path. So, don't be shy to ask. It's worth it.

At my live seminars we do powerful work in this area called Deserving Circles. I hope you get to experience this.

In addition, who knows what other resources these contacts may have that will help you on your path? They'll likely never offer if you don't ask. This is your life and your future. You don't have to do it all on your own.

*****

4. Your Personal Environment

Another way to strengthen your deserving belief is to be aware of your personal environment. Everything you see, hear, touch, taste, and smell stimulates your preconditioned thoughts every moment of your day. Because you are primarily in the same fixed environments (your home, car, office, neighborhood), the sensations you experience rarely change.

You drive to work on autopilot knowing every twist and turn. You could do it with your eyes closed. Whether it's getting out of bed, going to the bathroom, picking clothes from your closet, heading to the kitchen for breakfast or coffee, then walking to the garage to leave for work, you're always experiencing the exact same stimuli. This routine applies to your weekends, evenings, and holidays too.

Your entire life is a set of anticipated senses and stimuli influencing you. Each one produces a thought and a feeling. Since you're bombarded with hundreds of environmental cues around the clock, your brain filters them all into a conditioned stream of thought causing much of your attitude. The fixed sensations around you plus the thoughts, attitudes, and emotions, become a habit you've been exercising for years.

Remember, your emotions are primarily reactions to your experiences. This can be dangerous because most people have set themselves into negative or unconstructive mental patterns of feeling and thinking.

For instance, you get up in the morning five out of seven days of the week to go to a job you don't want to go to, without as much sleep as you wanted. You're groggy and a bit negative, but because it's been that way for ten years you don't notice how much it bothers you anymore. It feels normal to be tired in the morning and not full of optimism for the day. You couldn't imagine being excited and grateful for what a regular Monday has in store.

Then on weekend mornings you are woken up by kids earlier than you wanted or you have to get up to do something you'd rather not be doing (like going to your mother-in-law's home or mowing your lawn). You finish the day in your room exhausted, unfulfilled from the work and watch mindless TV before shutting off the lights to repeat the process tomorrow.

Over the years, the room in which you spend most of your life automatically produces feelings of lethargy and pessimistic thoughts like *"I wish I didn't have to do this today."* You may not feel those emotions or thoughts creeping up every time you walk into your room, but they are influencing you.

Does any environment in the routine of your life inspire you to feel excited, optimistic, joyful or grateful? Likely not. Or, maybe your favorite restaurant gives you that feeling for the first three minutes once you enter it once a month. You can become so conditioned to downer thoughts and emotions that you don't even notice them anymore because they are so prevalent in every aspect of your daily life.

This happens with our diets as well. A person who is unhealthy and eats fried food or ice cream often doesn't notice much difference in how their body feels over the next hour. Yet, someone who is healthy eats the same junk food and immediately feels tired and experiences an upset stomach or headache. Or maybe they become congested as an immune response from those unhealthy ingredients.

Consider this: You may be the unhealthy person not noticing the effects of the bad foods. Or, you may be numb, not noticing that each day you wake without enthusiasm.

Your surroundings don't just dictate your thoughts and feelings, they dictate your ability to see what is possible for your life.

When you flip your switch from undeserving to deserving one of the most significant advantages you'll start to see is your mind working in new ways, hatching new ideas to get what you want. In the past, if you didn't believe you deserved something, why would you receive ideas on how to get it? You wouldn't. When you believe you're deserving, you will.

How does this all relate to your environment? Your surroundings should not influence you in the wrong 'undeserving' direction. You don't want your home, office, and weekend routine to continually put you in an undeserving state of mind. Yet that's the state you have been in for the past five or twenty years, living in the exact same environment with similar routine and the same stimuli. So, what do you do when you cannot move homes or swap families or jobs easily (and I'm not alluding that your family or job is bringing you down or enforcing your undeserving belief)?

There are a few ways to address this issue without having to move across the country (although that option can certainly increase your deserving powerfully when done with the right intention). One idea is to address the personal spaces where you spend the most time—your home, office, and property. They all have a powerful effect on your deserving belief.

I love Marie Kondo's insightful book *The Life Changing Magic of Tidying Up*. In it, she teaches an extraordinarily simple approach to change your living space by ridding it of anything not bringing you joy. I endorse her methodology 100% as a way to *increase your deserving muscle*. The process she outlines (which when done correctly takes just one day) contributes to freeing you from past regret and fear of the future. Both of these emotions hinder your mind from optimism and joy. Her method also helps you see that you have more control over your life than you may believe.

So by taking inventory of all the physical objects in your environment and consciously removing ones that no longer serve you, you wipe the slate clean. You re-energize your physical environment, creating new space and room for more joy. Doing so starts the snowball effect, not just in your physical surroundings, but in more important decisions and life issues too.

I read her book even though I am a generally very tidy person who does not hold onto items I do not use. However, going through her process I found myself still filling three large garbage bags to throw out or give away just from inside my bedroom and closet.

Remember, putting this focus on your personal environment has little to do with a tidier home and everything to do with freeing you to move forward, creating the life you want.

* * * * *

5. What Are You Putting Up With?

Here's a simple exercise you can use today to start seeing a difference in your life. Think about every aspect of your daily weekday routine. Visualize your morning until your commute. Next, visualize your workday experience or however else you spend your weekdays. Lastly, see your commute home and your typical weekday evening.

While you're visualizing, see what part of this routine could be more inspiring. We become so habituated in our habits that we typically put up with a toothbrush that clearly needs replacing, breakfast foods that don't inspire, an often used gadget that needs fixing, the empty wall that needs a picture or, perhaps the absence of a really good book.

What element of life completely within your control are you putting up with? What things can you easily eliminate or replace? Yet you haven't done it because you are so stuck in your routine. This exercise serves by getting rid of what holds you back or doesn't foster an optimistic state of mind. It also builds the muscle that you have dominion over your environment and life. You have the power and control to make a change, even if you have been stuck in the old way for years.

By starting small it is more likely you'll act on it, see and feel a difference and have the momentum to continue with larger items and issues. I remember this showing up in my practice with my patient scheduling and appointment book. My team did everything in pencil because re-schedules and cancellations are very common and appointments need to be erased and rewritten into the master schedule book. Some pencils have truly awful erasers that seem to be wrapped in a thin plastic coating causing dark smudges everywhere when used…

Every time I looked at the schedule, it irritated me. It looked messy and unprofessional, and did not make me proud of a very important part of my business, making appointments to see my patients. And I put up with it until finally I decided that's enough. I left during lunch and bought brand new pencils with the best possible erasers that actually worked. I threw out all the current, even unused remaining ones. From then on I got to enjoy the simple pleasure of a clean appointment book.

This example may seem minuscule and silly to you, but we all have areas we put up with. We are often so close and accustomed to our routine and environment we don't even realize what we are putting up with. Each act of letting go of or changing what you are putting up with builds your deserving muscle. No matter how small the act, it demonstrates you standing up for and respecting your quality of life. Small acts lead to monumental changes.

Right now, stop for a second and think: What is one thing from your daily routine you have absolute control over and don't want to put up with any more? Just by acknowledging it and choosing you are now in control. Start small, with the tiniest items—maybe the quality of the coffee you drink or the song you switch to for your alarm clock or the choice to read something that brings you joy for three minutes before running out of the house to work. Just by making these choices you will start the ball rolling to build muscle for realizing that you *do* have a say in how your life feels.

There are countless areas in which you can make a worthwhile change when you simply stop and observe what you're doing and how it's serving you.

The more you shed what you don't want in life the clearer you will become about what you do want. You'll be rewarded with greater peace of mind and overall happiness. These choices will strengthen your deserving belief. If you're willing to put up with what you don't want every day of your life and not do something about it, it is highly doubtful you believe you deserve the life you dream of!

* * * * *

By nature, I'm frugal and conscious of every dollar I spend. This habit was ingrained in me by my mother who is also highly money conscious. I'd often hear her say, "I just have such a hard time spending money."

At any given moment, I'm able to tell you exactly how much money I have in my pocket and in my bank accounts.

When I see something for sale, I immediately think to myself, "Is this worth the price?" I know a water bottle is likely produced for three cents and when bought in bulk sells for about twenty cents. A typical store will sell the same bottle of water for one dollar. Therefore, I have become accustomed to a bottle of water being worth one dollar.

But not in New York City! It's common to pass by a hot dog vendor, and that same bottle of water is selling for two dollars. If it's at a concert it could be five dollars! I see the price and think, "How much is that really worth?" I am bothered it's being sold for far more than its normal retail price.

So, I often don't buy it even though it's a hot day, even though I'm thirsty, and two dollars won't make any difference to my net worth. I admit this is being crazy. I sacrifice my peace of mind and physical comfort out of righteousness over my perception of an item's value. But, I didn't just do this with water bottles. *I did this everywhere.* I would sacrifice experiences because of this mentality, not allowing myself to enjoy my life to the fullest —whether at restaurants, experiences with friends, or things I wanted.

Since coming to understand the impact a deserving belief has on every aspect of my life, I've now switched around the question I ask myself. I no longer wonder, "Is this worth it?" It's too easy to honestly answer, "No, it's not." And then I deny myself the experience.

Even though I may fully believe I deserve to have it, the decision to deprive myself of whatever it is (even with a logical reason) instills in me a feeling of lack. And, over time, these experiences build up and *produce a mentality of not deserving what I want.*

You may be doing this in your life too.

A profound shift occurred when I started to ask myself a new question about what I wanted. I now ask, "Do I *deserve* this?" Most often the answer is "YES." And more often now I choose to get it. I'm priming my mind for living a deserving life.

But when I look back on all the choices I've made about whether to purchase something I can see how the answer "NO" kept me from feeling deserving. However, when I switched my question to "Do I deserve this?" and get a "YES," I thereafter didn't regret any of my choices, even if there was less money in my pocket afterward.

There is nothing more important than how you feel emotionally, physically, and spiritually. A sense of well-being dictates everything you do and the quality with which you do it. So the most important priority in your life is how you feel on a daily basis. I believe you are inherently deserving of whatever it is you want.

So if you notice that you're asking self-sabotaging questions or making self-defeating statements, consider using the question, "Do I deserve this?" It can make all the difference to you.

Chapter 6 Most Important Takeaways

- The Deserving Process allows you to finally "flip your switch." The six steps allow you to strengthen your newfound belief.
- The frequency and quality with which you do these steps and The Deserving Process determines how strong your deserving belief becomes.
- There are numerous actions you can take to strengthen your deserving beliefs. Challenge yourself to do each one over the coming months alongside The Deserving Process daily.

End of Chapter 6

Workbook for Deservingness

Personal Reflection in each area of the deserving strengthening resources shared in this chapter:

1. Where can you see your current life reinforcing or keeping you stuck in an undeserving belief?
2. What can you apply from this chapter to strengthen your newfound deserving belief?

For example: "What You Are Putting Up With?"

a. I spend way too much time listening to my friends complain about finances and how unfair and tough their life is… The conversation never changes, it's draining to always listen to and a complete waste of time and it affects my own beliefs on how tough life can be.

b. I can choose not to engage in these conversations and enable my friends by listening and supporting the struggle. Instead I can be a resource for myself and my friends to improve our financial lives instead of staying stuck just complaining about it.

For each area write at least one (A) and one (B) to document how it appears in your life:

Your Daily Routine:
   A.
   B.

Your Personal Space:
   A.
   B.

Connecting With Deservers:
   A.
   B.

Hearing You Deserve It:
   A.
   B.

Deserving Question:
   A.
   B.

What You Are Putting Up With:
   A.
   B.

Conclusion

Your True Power

Congratulations! In this book, you've learned the most important question to ask, and you have gotten the answer which will lead you to get what you want in your life.

You have learned the process for creating what is truly important to you.

By flipping the switch to you *are* deserving, you are in a frame of mind that attracts abundance and happiness. And you finally realize that, all along, the biggest obstacle to your happiness was YOU. Now it is your choice to create your deserving beliefs.

This book is proof that we need to learn from others, that knowledge and wisdom is to be found within each of us and from those all around us. Indeed, you have learned the importance of connecting to a peer group of others—friends, mentors, and colleagues—who all share your values. Especially if their lives illustrate that they believe they deserved the best, and they encourage the same in you.

"But there's more to it than just deserving."

This is the final piece of the puzzle, the final component that will help you bring about more significant change in your life and in the lives of those you care most about.

As with many new discoveries, it takes practice to apply deserving beliefs before we can experience their full potential. I didn't see that at first. It was a chance conversation with a long-time patient who became a friend who helped me to see the full power of "gifting."

Matthew is a diverse and impressive man, an academic who writes books, teaches and studies philosophy, religion, and art. He's also an entrepreneur who runs a business and even finds time to mentor others. I recently had lunch with him one Friday afternoon in Manhattan and we decided to walk off our meal with a stroll through Central Park.

I shared the deserving belief concept with him and waited for what I hoped would be his enthusiastic response. Instead, there was dead silence. We walked on for several moments while he reflected on what I had said. I waited nervously. Matthew was more than a friend to me; he was a mentor and confidant. So his opinion mattered.

Finally, after what seemed like forever, he said, " we are interdependent, social beings. We do not live in isolation. Introspection is a necessary part of this process of growth, but for the truth-seeker who desires the very best for themselves, they must put this process into practice with others. *It will not work if your focus is entirely on self.* You must implement giving to others for this to become lasting in the lives of those you teach."

Matthew had, not surprisingly, touched on a simple but profound truth. Just as the deserving belief relies on implementing these truths into our own life through a proven process, the next step comes through giving away the deserving belief to others.

There is someone in your life who needs to hear that they deserve the life they want. They need to hear that the future they want is within their power to create by "flipping the switch." Be that voice for them. You likely also need to hear it yourself.

Share this book with that person today, not to change them for your benefit, but so they can change *themselves* for greater peace of mind and true happiness. They deserve it too!

When you selflessly give in this way, the act itself reinforces the belief in your own life. You cannot give to another what you don't have. You are building a stronger more deserving belief within your own subconscious every time you share this and contribute to a deserving belief in another.

A physical analogy might help; when you exercise with weight resistance, your muscles grow stronger. Indeed, repeated stress doesn't weaken them or cause them to shrivel up, but rather the exact opposite. It is much the same with your mind and your soul; the more you *flex* those muscles and the deeper your commitment to personal growth, the more powerful and long-lasting the deserving belief becomes *in* your life.

There is another benefit to sharing this gift with others, and that's the enrichment of your community. Many of us live in social environments with people who can be pessimistic and resigned. The people you surround yourself have a tremendous impact on how you feel about yourself and what you will do today, tomorrow and in the future.

Research shows that our own sense of self-worth is a direct result of how much we are valued by others in our social community.[1] This scientific truth is why we feel good when someone compliments us or tells us how important we are to them.

Just imagine a community of men and women who are positive, encouraging, and working to lift up those when in need. How much better would your life—and theirs—be if the environment were healthy, positive, and committed to progress towards happiness and fulfillment?

So, as you begin living your life in joy and gratitude (and with a true belief you deserve it), this becomes a first step towards building a community around you. How? By giving this book to someone who can and will use it.

Remember, you will always be aware of your past hardships, frustrations or suffering, but you are no longer a victim. Forgive those who have wronged you even if they have not apologized. This includes yourself. We all make mistakes. So forgive yourself, today, and free yourself from past mistakes. Because as long as you are unforgiving, the related undeserving emotion acts as an obstacle to your happiness.

You have so much to be grateful for, starting with the discovery of The Deserving Process. I promise that your life will become more peaceful, optimistic, and joyful when you practice this process. In time, your deserving belief will become habit.

No longer are you going to feel stuck or burned out. The feelings of resignation will begin to fade away. Once the deserving belief is part of your core you will naturally be taking the right steps that create the life you seek. You will carry it with you throughout every area of your life and *your new life will become a masterpiece of your own creation.* That is the potential you now have within you!

It has been the journey of a lifetime to be able to share this with you. I am grateful for every twist and turn in my life that made this possible. I appreciate the ups and downs, the people I've worked with and the relationships that I have built. As you read these words, I am certain that this knowledge and the process I've shared with you will awaken the realization that you ARE deserving. I believe you WILL "flip your switch."

I also invite you to join me in person at one of my upcoming seminars so we can progress together in a deeper understanding and strengthening of The Deserving Process. I'd love to meet you.

Let's do this together. You deserve it.

---

[1] Kawamichi et al. 2018

Printed in Great Britain
by Amazon